Greenwich Readers

Education & Training for Life

Professionalism, Policies and Values

This Reader is one of a series designed to support teachers and trainers in the post-compulsory sector of education. It will be of value to those who are working in colleges of further and higher education, sixth form colleges, adult and community education institutes, training units, and institutions of specific vocational preparation in the health service, the police service and the armed forces. The topics have been selected to represent a wide view of currently important issues and, by providing appropriate material for critical reflection on professional practice, the book will meet the needs of experienced teachers and trainers as well as those in the earlier stages of their careers.

In addition to such general use, the volume is one component of an integrated Certificate in Education/Postgraduate Certificate in Education course offered by the School of Post-Compulsory Education and Training at the University of Greenwich. Further information on this and other programmes of study and related academic services may be obtained from

School of PCET
University of Greenwich
30 Park Row
London SE10 9LS

telephone: 020 8331 9230
fax: 020 8331 9235
e-mail: pcet@gre.ac.uk
www.gre.ac.uk

The planned range of titles in this series is as follows:

- Adult Learners, Key Skills & the Post-16 Curriculum
- Equality, Participation & Inclusive Learning
- Flexible Learning & ICT

- Language, Communication & Learning
- Perspectives on Learning
- Planning Teaching & Assessing Learning
- Professionalism, Policies & Values
- Supporting Students

Enquiries about the current availability of these publications should be addressed to the School Office at the above address.

Tony Lewis
Series Editor

Professionalism, Policies and Values

A Reader

Lynda Hall
&
Ken Marsh

Published in 2000 by Greenwich University Press and prepared for publication by:

Procurement and Business Services Department
University of Greenwich
Woolwich University Campus
Wellington Street
London SE18 6PF

ISBN 1 86166 074 X

Cover designed by Pete Birkett

Text design and layout by Christine Murray

In the majority of cases the contents of the readings and extracts in this volume have been reproduced as they appear in the publications from which they have been taken.

Every effort has been made to trace all the copyright holders, but if any have inadvertently been overlooked the publishers will be pleased to make the necessary arrangements at the earliest opportunity.

University of Greenwich, a charity and a company limited by guarantee, registered in England (reg no 986729). Registered Office: 30 Park Row, Greenwich, London SE10 9LS.

Contents

Acknowledgements

Acknowledgement is made for permission to reproduce the extracts and diagrams quoted:

Ainley P & Bailey B (1997) *The business of learning: staff and student experiences of further education in the 1990s* Cassell, pp14–18; 23

Beaty L (1997) 'Becoming a professional teacher in higher education' in *Developing your teaching through reflective practice SEDA Special no 5* Staff and Educational Development Association, pp7–11; 'Ethical principles in university teaching' *op cit*, Appendix A

Church of England Board of Education (1993) *A framework for exploring values in the FE curriculum*, pp1–9; 11–17; 19–20 (Board of Education and Church House Publishing, 1993) are copyright © The Archbishops' Council and are reproduced by permission

Ecclestone K (1996) 'The reflective practitioner: mantra or a model for emancipation?' *Studies in the Education of Adults* 28 (2), pp149–152; 154–156; 158

Evans K, Hodkinson P, Keep E, Rainbird R, Senker P, Sutherland J & Unwin L (1999) *Working to learn: is New Labour learning? A critique of New Labour's policies for work-related learning* Paper presented to ESRC Seminar at the Institute of Education, London, 19.11.99

Fullerton H (1993) 'Observation of teaching: guidelines for observers and observed' in S Brown, G Jones & S Rawnsley *Observing Teaching SCED Paper 79* Standing Conference on Educational Development, pp78–82

Gibbs G (1988) *Learning by doing – a guide to teaching & learning methods* FEU, pp9–10; diagram from p104; checklist from p106

Huddlestone P & Unwin L (1997) 'The employment perspective' in G Stanton & W Richardson (eds) *Qualifications for the future: a study of tripartite and other divisions in post-16 education and training* FEDA, pp143–169

Hughes M (1985) 'Leadership in professionally staffed organisations' in M Hughes, P Ribbins & H Thomas (eds) *Managing education: the system and the institution* Holt, Rinehart and Winston, pp269–272

O'Neill M & Pennington G (1992) 'Evaluating teaching and courses from an active learning perspective Part 1' in *Effective learning and teaching in higher education* CVCP Universities' Staff Development and Training Unit, figures 2, 3a & 3b from pp39–41; pp35–37

Randle K & Brady N (1997) 'Managerialism and professionalism in the "Cinderella service"' *Journal of Vocational Education & Training* 49 (1), pp121–139

Robson J (1998) 'A profession in crisis: status, culture and identity in the further education college' in *Journal of Vocational Education and Training* 50 (4), pp585–591; 593–4; 596–7; 602–3

Stanton G (1997) 'Patterns in development' in S Tomlinson (ed) *Education 14–19: critical perspectives* The Athlone Press, pp37–54

The School of Post-Compulsory Education and Training

The School of PCET, as it is known, has its origin in Garnett College in London, one of three institutions set up by the Ministry of Education in the late 1940s for the initial training of technical college lecturers. After many developments and organisational changes over the past 50 years, its future within the University of Greenwich will be from a campus on the banks of the River Thames in Christopher Wren's former Royal Naval College.

The School's services and students, though, are not only locally based, but nationwide and international. PCET is a leader in distance provision for lecturers, trainers, administrators and other support staff from all sectors of post-school provision, as well as from the public services and voluntary and commercial training organisations. It has associated centres in various parts of the United Kingdom, and there are projects in China, South Africa and Russia, and leadership of research and information networks within the European Union.

We aim, in both our teaching and our research, to relate professional practice to learning theory and current policy issues. This permeates all of the School's programmes – from initial training on Cert Ed/PGCE programmes, through professional development at BA/BSc and Masters levels and the work of our Training and Development Office, to our portfolio of short courses and bespoke in-house provision. There is a thriving group of research students, and the School has been at the forefront of innovation in computer mediated communication. We provide a comprehensive service for further, higher and adult education, helping people to help others learn through life.

Ian McNay
Head of School

Lynda Hall taught Computing and IT in a further education college for a number of years before becoming involved in teacher education at the University of Greenwich. She specialises in the teaching of IT skills and in training future teachers of IT. A current responsibility is running the attendance mode of the part-time in-service Certificate in Education/PGCE at Greenwich.

Ken Marsh is Senior Lecturer in Policy and Comparative Studies in the School of PCET. He is active in European work, being European co-ordinator for the School, a former chair of the Vocational Teacher Training Group of the Association of Teachers and Educators in Europe, and currently the UK representative of the European Training of Trainers Network at the European Centre for the Development of Vocational Training. He represents the University of Greenwich on the University Council for the Education of Teachers (UCET) European Committee.

Introduction

This Reader has been compiled to give teachers and trainers, both in the early stages of their professional careers in post-compulsory education and training and later, a framework for reflecting on and evaluating the core professional activities of all teachers and trainers. The later contributions place this view of professionalism within the context of the political and social environment of education and training, and so give an insight into the policies and values within which we all operate.

Part One explores the concept of professionalism. We have no difficulty in classifying lawyers and doctors as being 'professionals'. But what are our criteria for making this judgement? How far can we say – and how far would other people agree – that teachers, trainers and lecturers are also fully professional people? And what about social workers and nurses? Is there something in the entry processes, in the training, in the culture and behaviour expected in these vocational areas that makes us speak of them as professions? Section 1 tries to answer some of these questions, and considers the management issues associated with the employment of professionals in bureaucratic institutions like colleges and universities. The next contribution addresses some of the more vexing features of working in the post-16 sector today, and this Part ends with an exploration of a number of the specific duties and moral responsibilities of all those who are employed as teachers.

Part Two introduces the theme of continuing professional development and the idea of the 'reflective practitioner' as one who accepts the responsibility of continuously learning from experience during the progress of a teaching career. The concept and the practice of reflection as a deliberate professional activity are analysed in some detail, and explanations given of how teachers can learn from their experiences and gather information on their practice through regular self assessment and peer observations. But reflective practice is itself a contested concept, and some of the contrary arguments are presented in the last section of this Part.

We all have to work within the constraints imposed by external forces, not only those arising from the policy decisions made at local, regional, national and indeed international levels, but also those which derive from the pressures of social and institutional cultures and of the sets of values which lie behind them. Part Three provides an account of the emergence of central government interest in the post-school sector from the years after the second world war right up to the implementation of current legislation. The contributions will make it all too clear why it is commonly described as the 'Cinderella sector', and the main feature of the past fifty years is shown to be the lack of coherence in the development of policy.

Part Four explores the particular context of the world of work and vocational training, and the story is strangely familiar as it reveals the continuing inability of successive governments to trust the professional teachers and trainers. The first two sections in this Part present a detailed – sometimes hilarious – account of political decision-making on employment and training during the Conservative years of the 1980s and 1990s. The final section will remind us of the importance of studying the policies and practices of the past, and of the depressing truth that few politicians seem to learn from this activity.

In Part Five we attempt to bring these various threads together with an account of how recent policies and political actions have affected what professional teachers and trainers actually do within their institutions. The readings conclude with an all-too-rare attempt to identify and explore those shared values which seem to inform the progressive development of the institutions, the curricula, the staff and the students.

We hope that the contributions in this volume will give important insights into the current condition of professionals working in the post-school sector and of the institutions within which we work. Though a number of the sections focus specifically on vocational education and training we believe that they are relevant to all professionals in the post-school sector – one way of protecting our professionalism is to be widely informed on all matters associated with political decision-making.

Lynda Hall & Ken Marsh
April 2000

Part One – The Concept of Professionalism

The theme of this Part is that the trade of the teacher and trainer is one that shares with doctors, dentists, lawyers, accountants and architects the qualities of being a 'profession'. However, this is a view that is not accepted by all commentators, and certainly some would argue that 'real' professional people do not have trade unions as teachers do, and neither do they get treated by the agents of Government in the way that has been evident in recent decades of increasingly centralised management control over staff in schools and colleges.

There is much evidence that the role and status of teachers in society has diminished over the years, and the move to employ minimally trained assessors and instructors in colleges, and to delegate the employment of part-timers to commercial agencies, makes it necessary to re-assert a belief in the proper designation of teaching as a professional activity. In the first contribution Meredydd Hughes surveys the research on what it means to be a professional, and considers the implications for those organisations which employ such people. The new 'managerialism' is perhaps not sympathetic to the demands and expectations of a work-force of trained, independent, self-actualising professional people. This theme re-emerges in the article by Keith Randle and Norman Brady which constitutes Section 16 in Part Five.

In the second extract Jocelyn Robson argues that further education teachers in particular have low status, low levels of professional autonomy and no clear professional identity. She attributes this to a number of factors: the lack of the requirement for formal teacher training for those working or seeking to work in the sector; the diversity of entry routes into FE teaching and the consequential weak professional boundaries; the lack of coherence and consensus about the work of FE teachers; and conflicting occupational identities amongst them. FE has often been called the 'Cinderella' of the education system. Are FE teachers the 'Cinderellas' of the teaching profession?

One of the characteristics of a profession is what Barber (quoted by Hughes) called 'control through a code of ethics emanating from a voluntary association'. Teachers, unlike other professionals such as doctors and lawyers, do not have – for the moment at least – a single controlling professional body nor an agreed code of ethics.

However, most educational establishments do have policies relating to equal opportunities, and a disciplinary code. The majority of teachers would probably agree about what constitutes 'unprofessional' conduct or unethical practice. Nevertheless, currently there is no explicit set of principles to guide the practice of all teachers. Should there be? Would teachers benefit from this?

The contributions by Liz Beaty – written for university teachers, but equally applicable to all those working in the post-16 sector – remind us of our commitment to an unwritten code of professional ethics and of our responsibilities to ourselves, our students, our colleagues and our institutions. The two brief extracts explore in very practical terms the continuing and continuous process of reflective practice, and present a set of nine 'basic ethical principles' which we might wish to use to inform all our work in education and training.

1. Professionals and the Management of Organisations

Meredydd Hughes

In this section consideration will first be given to the different views which have been expressed concerning the nature of professionalism, earlier assumptions concerning essential characteristics of professions being more recently questioned. The implications for organisational management of employing a professional work-force will then be considered, including the potential for conflict and how such conflict can be resolved or avoided.

The concept of professionalism

Profession, like leadership, is an elusive concept and is a word with variations of meaning in the social science literature and even more so in general usage. Millerson (1964: 5) noted 23 distinct traits which have been included in various definitions of the term profession. According to Goode (1960), many of the characteristics that have been proposed are derivative, the two core characteristics in his view being a lengthy period of training in a body of abstract knowledge and a strong service orientation. Elsewhere he described the characteristics of a professional community as a sense of identity associated with shared values, an agreed role definition, a common technical language, and a recognition that the professional group has power over its members (Goode, 1957: 194–209). His work may be cited as an example of sociological studies which tended to accept, somewhat uncritically, the rhetoric of prominent professional groups and their unduly idealistic self-definitions of their special characteristics. As Johnson (1972: 25) has aptly observed, 'while the service ethic may be an important part of the ideology of many professional groups, it is not so clear that practitioners are necessarily so motivated'.

In contrast to the 'trait' approach adopted, though in a compressed form, by Goode, Barber looked for characteristics of professionalism which might be regarded as having functional relevance for the relationship of professional to client or for society generally. He identified four such characteristics: a high degree of systematic knowledge, orientation to community interest, control through a code of ethics emanating from a voluntary association, and a system of rewards which is 'primarily a set of symbols of work achievement' (Barber, 1963: 72). The underlying assumption that there is a universally recognised community interest, which is distinctively served by highly qualified occupational groups whose members are expected to place symbolic rewards above monetary gain, and generally do so, is one which may understandably give rise to scepticism, as Jackson (1970: 8) has noted. In a later definition of professional behaviour Barber (1978: 601) essentially retained the first three characteristics but made no reference to symbolic rewards.

A consistent advocate of a more critical approach to professionalism has been Everett Hughes, who cogently argued that the available evidence indicated that 'the concept "professional" in all societies is not so much a descriptive term as one of value and prestige' (Hughes, 1958: 44). He later proposed that attention should be given to the empirical question of how professionalised certain occupations are at a particular time, rather than seeking to determine whether they are professions in some absolute sense (Hughes, 1963). He was followed by Ben-David (1963–64), who analysed professions in relation to the class system of different societies, and Prandy (1965), who examined professional associations as status bodies which bestow a qualification and seek to maintain and enhance its prestige. Oleson & Whitaker (1970: 184), in a review of studies of professional socialisation, conclude that there is a tendency 'to overlook major discrepancies between the symbol of profession and the everyday human realities on which it rests'. In a similar realistic vein, Larson (1977: xvi) saw professionalisation as 'the process by which producers of special services sought to constitute *and control* a market for their expertise'.

Hall followed up his previous study of the elements of bureaucracy ... by a similar dimensional approach to professionalism. He examined the structural aspects of 27 professions and the attitudes expressed by their members, and found significant discrepancies between structural and attitudinal scores (Hall, 1969: 87–8, Table 4.2). Professionalised occupations structurally did not rank as highly as some others in terms of belief in service to the public or of sense of calling to the field. They invariably had the highest ranks, however, in terms of belief in self-regulation and the use of the professional organisation as a reference group.

The structures and procedures within professions which ensure a substantial measure of professional autonomy and control are increasingly being vigorously challenged by those who use professional services, as Barber (1978) and Wirt (1981) have clearly shown. Wirt has provided an instructive developmental model of political conflict between professionals and non-professionals, i.e. 'the laity'. He distinguishes five phases as follows: *quiescence,* which entails professional dominance; *issue emergence,* involving a growing number of random individual complaints by clients; *turbulence,* characterised by strong challenges and militant pressure groups, and in some cases by the emergence of 'inside agitators' within the professional ranks; *resolution,* the phase in which both the professional and lay representatives are engaged in vigorous debate and action, and which may also involve government as mediator or adjudicator; and finally *closure,* signifying the reduction of conflict as the professionals typically accept some redefinition of professional services, whether voluntarily or as a result of legally imposed constraints.

Wirt's illustrative examples relate mainly to medical and legal services in the USA, but he also includes apposite references to parental concern and governmental intervention in education in both the USA and the UK. The resulting involvement of professionals in external political activity, both at a micro level and at group level, albeit in a non-party sense in most cases, is well documented in Wirt's paper.

This brief review may be summed up with the observation that the early phases of Wirt's developmental model appear to be relevant to the concept of professionalism itself. The period up to about 1960 was largely one of quiescence, when the self perceptions of the professionals themselves, reinforced by their professional associations, were largely accepted not only by the relevant client groups but also by most social scientists. The 1960s and early 1970s may be regarded as a period of issue emergence, when the rhetoric of the professions began to be questioned, first by social science academics and then, in more robust terms, by individual clients and client groups. Since the mid-1970s there has clearly been a period of turbulence when the challenges are stronger and more co-ordinated, and some of the professional groups are themselves more active and vociferous in defending their interests, younger professionals themselves sometimes schizophrenically challenging established practice. Politicking flourishes, and there is little sign as yet of an abatement of conflict between the seemingly elitist aspirations of professionals and a widespread populist revolt which receives encouragement from radicals of both the political left and the political right. At the general level under consideration it appears that Wirt's final categories, resolution and closure, are difficult to envisage, being quite remote from the practical politics of life today.

Factors conducive to conflict within organisations

Professionals employed in organisations are liable to have difficulties from time to time in their relationships, not only with their clients or the public at large, but also with those in authority in their employing organisation. Professionals, it has been claimed, are unreasonably resistant to administrative control (Abrahamson, 1967).

Studies of scientists in research establishments (Hall & Lawler, 1970), studies of doctors and nurses in hospitals and clinics (Engel, 1970; Corwin, 1961), studies of social workers in local authority departments (Jordan, 1979; Glastonbury & Cooper, 1982), studies of accountants in large commercial firms (Sorenson & Sorenson, 1974), studies of teachers and lecturers in schools and colleges (Corwin, 1965; Noble & Pym, 1970) all share a common characteristic. They display similar patterns of latent or actual conflict between the occupational group and organisational requirements which cannot be simply explained away in terms of the recalcitrance of awkward individuals. The real issue, it appears, in the ubiquitous strain between professions and organisations is the relationship 'between two institutions, not merely between organisations and individuals' (Kornhauser, 1963: 8).

Areas of conflict have been comprehensively reviewed on a number of occasions (Scott, 1965; Etzioni, 1969; Harries-Jenkins, 1970; Rotondi, 1975; Larson, 1977). Many aspects have been discussed, Etzioni for instance suggesting that teachers, social workers and nurses might appropriately be regarded as semi-professionals on the two assumptions that they are more amenable than other professionals to bureaucratisation and that a higher proportion of them are women. The suggestion that these two assumptions are interconnected has been vigorously challenged (Neuse, 1978: 440), and the concept of semi-professionalism has largely been discarded, having proved to be even more elusive than that of professionalism itself.

Returning to the main theme, one can broadly distinguish in the literature between problems related to the professional's claim to autonomy within the organisation, and problems arising as a result of his or her external orientation and affiliations.

The professional's claim to autonomy

Because of their specialised training, professionals expect to be accorded a large measure of discretion in dealing with matters considered to be within their area of expertise. It is argued that it is by using their trained judgement in professional matters that they can best contribute to the objectives of their employing organisation. If they are employed in a highly structured, tight bureaucracy, a certain level of endemic conflict, erupting from time to time in major incidents, appears to be an almost inevitable consequence, as evidenced by research in different contexts.

A comprehensive study by Hall (1968) provides support for the proposition that the professional's quest for autonomy is the professional value which causes most difficulty in organisations. The research included doctors, nurses, lawyers, accountants, social workers and teachers. Bureaucratisation scales were developed for the organisational units within which the various professionals worked, and measures were obtained of attitudes towards professional values such as service to the public and sense of autonomy. Whereas other relationships proved to be relatively weak, Hall found a strong negative relationship between 'feeling of autonomy' and each of his five bureaucratic dimensions, namely, hierarchy of authority, division of labour, rules, procedures, and impersonality. He concluded that increased bureaucratisation threatens professional autonomy. The strong professional drive for autonomy, he noted, 'may come into direct conflict with organisationally based job requirements. At the same time the organisation may be threatened by strong professional desires on the part of at least some of its members' (Hall, 1968: 102–3).

A related issue is the professional's reluctance to accept without qualification the legitimacy of a hierarchy of authority. Professionals are well aware that technical expertise does not necessarily increase with position in the formal hierarchy. The extent of resistance to hierarchical control varies according to circumstances, ... the availability of appeal and consultative procedures being a significant factor. The quality of the professional commitment at the different organisational levels seems also to make a difference. Thus Scott (1965) found that social workers who regarded their supervisors as professionally oriented were less hostile to routine supervision than those who designated their supervisors as less professional, the supervision being acceptable when seen as an opportunity for helpful guidance by a senior colleague. On the other hand it was the more professionally oriented workers who were generally more critical of the control system than their less professionally motivated colleagues. A similar polarisation of attitude has been found among teachers and lecturers, identified by Corwin (1965) as a difference between *professional* and *employee* orientations, which is of relevance to the discussion of leadership in education...

The professional's external orientation

The second basic factor which tends to create problems is that the ideal stereotype of a professional establishes him or her as an incorrigible cosmopolitan. In a study of professionals in public agencies, Reissman (1949: 309) found that, in contrast to other employees, the professionals had a strong tendency 'to face outwards and away from the bureaucratic structure of their organisation'. With the accelerating increase of knowledge in all specialisms, the external aspect of professionalism has steadily increased in importance, familiarity with current professional literature and contact with colleagues across organisational boundaries being essential for the maintenance of standards and the further development of expertise. By such means professional credibility is retained and renewed, but this may sometimes be at the expense of the immediate organisational task. It is not surprising that frustrated, locally based administrators, who have to be concerned with the mundane task of organisation maintenance, become sceptical about the priorities and organisational loyalty of professional staff. Such differences of perspective are commonplace, for instance, in universities...

A notable pioneering study in this area was carried out by Gouldner (1957), who studied three aspects of the role orientation of the staff of a liberal arts college. He found that a high commitment to professional skills was positively related to an outside reference group orientation, and that both were negatively related to loyalty to the employing organisation as indicated by a wish to remain indefinitely in the organisation. Adopting a distinction drawn by Merton (1957) between *cosmopolitan* and *local* community leaders, Gouldner defined as 'cosmopolitan' the members of an organisation high in commitment to specialist skills and strongly oriented to outside reference groups, but low in organisational loyalty. The 'locals' were opposite in each respect. There is tension, Gouldner concluded, between an organisation's instrumental need for expertise which is provided by the cosmopolitans and its social need for loyalty which is provided by the locals.

Whereas the idea of a single cosmopolitan–local continuum of role orientations has had a powerful influence on later writers, Gouldner's assumption that his three variables, professional commitment, reference group orientation and organisational commitment, were so highly associated that they formed a single continuum was only partially supported by his research findings. Subsequent research has clearly demonstrated that the cosmopolitan–local typology is an over-simplification (Grimes & Berger, 1970) and that at the very least one must consider two independent dimensions, related respectively to professional commitment (or cosmopolitan orientation) and to organisational commitment (or local orientation). In addition to Gouldner's 'cosmopolitans' and 'locals', a two-dimensional model thus envisages two further categories, the 'cosmopolitan-locals' (i.e. those high on both dimensions), and the 'indifferents' (i.e. those low on both dimensions). That many persons do in fact manage to combine loyalty to their profession and to their organisation has been repeatedly shown in empirical research (Blau & Scott, 1963; Corwin, 1965; Thornton, 1970; Goldberg, 1976; Jauch *et al.* 1978). Goldberg showed, additionally, that commitment to organisational goals could be an incentive to professionals to increase their professional expertise.

While recent research has thus shown that it is misleading and unhelpful to automatically equate professionalism with disloyalty to the organisation, it is equally important not to lose sight of the fact that the insight of Reissman and Gouldner retains at least partial validity. It has to be accepted that, if professional expertise is to be credible and relevant in the modern world, a cosmopolitan, outward-looking stance is an essential element in the role orientation of professionals in organisations. Like the claim to autonomy, however, it is liable to give rise to tensions and problems in organisations which employ professionals.

References

Abrahamson M (1967) *The professional in the organisation* Rand McNally

Barber B (1963) 'Some problems in the sociology of the professions' *Daedalus* 92, pp669–88

Barber B (1978) 'Control and responsibility in the powerful professions' *Political Science Quarterly* 93, pp599–615

Ben-David J (1963–64) 'Professions in the class system of present-day societies: a trend report and bibliography' *Current Sociology* 12, pp247–330

Blau PM & Scott WR (1963) *Formal organisations: a comparative approach* Routledge & Kegan Paul

Corwin RG (1961) 'The professional employee: a study of conflict in nursing roles' *American Journal of Sociology* 66, pp604–15

Corwin RG (1965) 'Militant professionalism, initiative and compliance in public education' *Sociology of Education* 38, pp310–31

Engel GV (1970) 'Professional autonomy and bureaucratic organisation' *Administrative Science Quarterly* 51, pp50–60

Etzioni A (1969) *Modern organisations* Prentice-Hall

Glastonbury B & Cooper DM (1982) 'Case studies of bureaucratisation' in B Glastonbury *et al. Social work in conflict* British Association of Social Workers

Goldberg AI (1976) 'The relevance of cosmopolitan/local orientations to professional values and behaviour' *Sociology of Work and Occupations* 3, pp331–56

Goode WJ (1957) 'Community within a community: the profession' *American Sociological Review* 22, pp194–200

Goode WJ (1960) 'Encroachment, charlatanism and the emerging professions: psychology, sociology and medicine' *American Sociological Review* 25, pp902–13

Gouldner AW (1957) 'Cosmopolitans and locals: towards an analysis of latent social roles: I and II' *Administrative Science Quarterly* 2, pp281–306 and 444–80

Grimes AJ & Berger PK (1970) 'Cosmopolitan-local: evaluation of the construct' *Administrative Science Quarterly* 15, pp407–16

Hall DT & Lawler EE (1970) 'Job characteristics and pressures and the organisational integration of professionals' *Administrative Science Quarterly* 12, pp461–78

Hall RH (1968) 'Professionalisation and bureaucratisation' *American Sociological Review* 33 (1), pp92–104

Hall RH (1969) *Occupations and the social structure* Prentice-Hall.

Harries-Jenkins G (1970) 'Professionals in organisations' in JA Jackson (ed) *Professions and professionalisation* Cambridge University Press

Hughes EC (1958) *Men and their work* The Free Press

Hughes EC (1963) 'Professions' *Daedalus* 92, pp655–8

Jackson JA (ed) (1970) *Professions and professionalisation* Cambridge University Press

Jauch LR, Glueck WF & Osborn RN (1978) 'Organisational loyalty, professional commitment and academic research productivity' *Academy of Management Journal* 21, pp84–92

Johnson TJ (1972) *Professions and power* Macmillan

Jordan B (1979) *Helping in social work* Routledge & Kegan Paul

Kornhauser W (1963) *Scientists in industry: conflict and accommodation* University of California Press

Larson MS (1977) *The rise of professionalism* University of California Press

Merton RK (1957) *Social theory and social structure* rev edn The Free Press

Millerson G (1964) *The qualifying associations: a study in professionalisation* Routledge & Kegan Paul

Neuse SM (1978) 'Professionalism and authority: women in public service' *Public Administration Review* 38 (5), pp436–41

Noble T & Pym B (1970) 'Collegial authority and the receding locus of power' *British Journal of Sociology* 21, pp431–45

Oleson V & Whitaker EW (1970) 'Critical notes on sociological studies of professional socialisation' in JA Jackson (ed) *Professions and professionalisation* Cambridge University Press

Prandy K (1965) *Professional employees: a study of scientists and engineers* Faber

Reissman L (1949) 'A study of role conceptions in bureaucracy' *Social Forces* 27, pp305–10

Rotondi T (1975) 'Organisational identification: issues and implications' *Organisational Behaviour and Human Performance* 13, pp95–109

Scott WR (1965) 'Reactions to supervision in a heterogeneous professional organisation' *Administrative Science Quarterly* 10, pp65–81

Sorensen JE & Sorensen TL (1974) 'The conflict of professionals in bureaucratic organisations' *Administrative Science Quarterly* 19, pp98–106

Thornton R (1970) 'Organisational involvement and commitment to organisation and profession' *Administrative Science Quarterly* 15, pp417–26

Wirt F (1981) 'Professionalism and political conflict: a developmental model' *Journal of Public Policy* 1(1), pp61–93

2. A Profession in Crisis: Status, Culture and Identity in the Further Education College

Jocelyn Robson

Introduction

The further education teaching profession is currently in a state of crisis. After decades of official neglect, the Further and Higher Education Act (1992), the first major legislation to focus directly on Further Education (FE) since the war, has significantly raised the profile of the sector, but it has so far done little to improve the standing of the professional group as a whole. The Act has precipitated some massive shifts in the FE workplace and its culture, but to many of those working in it, these legislative changes and the unaccustomed attention of the state have been unwelcome. Their professional lives have been radically altered as a result and many feel that the changes have not been for the better (e.g. see Ainley & Bailey, 1997).

To many outside education, FE teachers appear as an anomalous group, with an ambivalent status and an unclear identity. No doubt many professional groups would have had difficulty withstanding the kinds of pressures that have been brought about by the Act, but it will be argued here that the FE teaching profession may have been particularly vulnerable, not for reasons that have to do with the competence or commitment of its members, but because of its history, its composition and its marginality within the educational system as a whole.

The fact is that the FE teaching profession has made little progress over the last 100 years towards full professional status. Why should this be so? What particular features of the profession are obstacles to its advancement, to what sociologists would call its 'professional project' (Macdonald, 1995)...

Profile of the work-force

... By 1979 about 45% of all full-time staff (and fewer part-time staff) in what was ... a diversified 'further education' sector possessed a recognised teaching qualification. By this time, the number of full-time teachers had increased to at least 60,000 (Cantor & Roberts [1986] put the 1980 figure at about 80,000). Though the available figures are not always directly comparable, it seems clear that as Young et al. conclude (on the basis of DfE statistics), there was a steady increase in the proportion of qualified staff in colleges from the mid-1970s through the 1980s (Young et al. 1995). By the early 1990s, this trend was in danger of being reversed, however, as colleges sought to increase the number of part-timers recruited mostly in order to cope with funding pressures. Since part-time staff are less likely to be trained than full-timers, the overall proportion of qualified teachers seems set to fall. Though the current estimate is that approximately 60% of full-time teaching staff in the FE sector now possess a recognised teaching qualification (Young et al. 1995), this is accounted for partly by the inclusion in 1993 of the sixth form colleges. The number of full-time opportunities is decreasing, with some colleges now employing part-timers to teach as much as 50% of their work (FEFC, 1997).

The broad picture, therefore, is of a sector which has grown dramatically in numerical terms over the last few decades, but in which it has not seemed possible to implement a consistent policy with regard to the status of its staff. The proportion of part-time staff (with their marginality and their lower rewards) has fluctuated in response to structural and policy change as has the proportion of all staff who are teacher-trained. It now seems likely that a formal teaching qualification will soon become mandatory (as the Dearing report has recommended for the higher education sector in the United Kingdom [DfEE, 1997]), but large questions remain about the nature of this training and the form that it might take, as well as about its consequent status.

With regard to the vocational and technical qualifications which staff were required to have, here, too, there is little uniformity. As a UNESCO report on technical and vocational teacher education noted, there is a great variety of qualifications accepted or considered appropriate for vocational and technical teachers in all countries (UNESCO, 1973), and in the United Kingdom these range from university degrees, higher diplomas, membership of professional or chartered institutes to the appropriate City and Guilds' certificates. According to DfE statistics quoted in Young *et al.* (1995), in 1991 about 48% of full-time FE teachers were graduates. The huge diversity of professional and vocational qualifications which is to be found amongst the staff in any college is symptomatic, of course, of the labyrinthine nature of technical and vocational education itself; the 'jungle' of qualifications that the National Council for Vocational Qualifications (NCVQ) was in part set up to rationalise (DES/DOE, 1985) still persists, certainly amongst those old enough to have sufficient industrial or commercial experience to enter further education teaching.

The very diversity of entry routes into FE teaching, however, creates, in sociological terms, a weak professional boundary. According to the Weberian concept of social closure, groups which have an interest to pursue, however those groups have originated, will typically endeavour to achieve monopoly and to close economic and social opportunities to outsiders (Macdonald, 1995). Generally, within one occupational area of the FE curriculum, it would probably be possible to specify quite clearly the level and nature of required entry qualifications for staff, but for the sector as a whole, these are so varied as to make closure very limited. School teachers, on the other hand, must be graduates to enter the profession and, despite increasingly diverse forms of 'graduateness', this professional 'gate' exists, effectively protecting the interests of members and enhancing the profession's status (relative, at least, to further education). This is not an argument for making FE teaching a graduate only profession; since degrees are not available in many of the vocational subjects offered in FE, this would be wholly inappropriate and quite unworkable. It is simply a further illustration of the profession's fragmentation. There are effectively hundreds of routes in and any number of professional 'boundaries'. The combined effect of a lack of any requirement to be teacher trained and this enormous diversity in vocational and technical entry routes is to weaken the profession's standing overall quite considerably.

In addition, there is not and never has been any attempt to control centrally the numbers entering FE teaching. In 1944, the McNair Report noted that 'in the main, the methods of recruitment of technical teachers have been haphazard and opportunist and as yet nothing systematic is being done to provide for the needs of the future' (Board of Education, 1944: 112), and this is still the case. Again, the contrast can be drawn with school teaching where successive governments have attempted (not always successfully) to predict demand and to control supply. With no means of controlling numbers and no means of planning national provision, the FE sector is effectively deprived of a further key strategy for enhancing its status – that of controlling the numbers seeking entry to its teaching profession. Professional exclusivity is indeed low and likely to become even lower, with the increasing tendency for colleges to blur the distinction between teaching and non-teaching staff (Young *et al.* 1995).

One further point should be made in relation to FE teachers' backgrounds, and that concerns the way they and others have consistently prioritised their industrial or commercial experiences (over, for instance, a teacher training qualification)...

... Fears about losing touch with one's professional or vocational background are real and understandable (especially amongst full-timers) and it is ironical that despite the importance attached in that report to vocational experience, McNair's recommendation ... that regular return to industry should be facilitated, so that technical teachers could refresh their knowledge and skills, has never been implemented...

Nature of the work

... The nature of teaching in FE has always varied enormously and continues to vary within the different curriculum areas. As the sector has expanded its provision, so its character has become more complex and the demands upon teachers have increased...

After describing a number of changes which have affected the work of FE teachers since the 1960s, the author continues.

There is [a] significant curriculum shift currently underway which is worth mentioning here, for it has clear implications for the FE teacher's role and relationships. This is the development of a variety of forms of flexible learning, such as the use of distance materials, drop-in workshops, computer-mediated communication and so on. The need for colleges to become cost-effective (even before incorporation) was leading to the development of more open and adaptable systems of learning and to an emphasis on access (Stanton, 1989). With incorporation and new funding imperatives, these trends have been accelerated.

Students enrolled in flexible programmes of various kinds need to take more responsibility for their own learning and teachers need strategies for ensuring that their students acquire sufficient confidence and autonomy (Ware, 1996). Though such skills have always been required of FE lecturers, the stakes are higher now for the colleges, and managers are increasingly seeking to develop and reward professional flexibility and innovation.

Overall, a picture is emerging here in which the FE teacher's work appears to be extremely variable and highly susceptible to change...

Sometimes it has been government policy or legislation that has precipitated the change; sometimes it has been the way policy has been implemented by the central agencies; sometimes the shifts have been precipitated by broader economic or social adjustments, or changes in awareness and priorities. Seldom has the change seemed to come from the sector itself; seldom has there been a successful attempt by the FE professionals themselves to define and demarcate the boundaries of their work.

Viewed from the outside, the lack of coherence and consensus about the nature of the FE teacher's professional work is particularly obvious and the degree of overlap with other professional roles (such as librarian or counsellor) is increasing. The pushes and pulls that the sector has been subject to have impacted here most significantly of all, and have certainly contributed to a further weakening of professional boundaries (such as they exist at all) and to continuing low levels of professional autonomy. The profession is not clearly demarcated and has not achieved a specialised or protected title. It has been reduced to trying to fend off draconian increases in hours and weeks, to what is effectively a proletarian struggle, when the real battle for professional status lies elsewhere...

Cultures in the college

... Not surprisingly, this diversity in the backgrounds of FE teachers and in the nature of the work they undertake leads to the development of a number of quite distinctive cultures, often within one college...

In moving from one occupational area (in industry or commerce) to another (education and training), most further education teachers retain strong allegiances to their first occupational identity. As noted above, this identity is what gives them credibility (as well as knowledge and skill) and it is therefore understandable that much value attaches to it. They have experienced initial occupational or professional socialisation in one context, and are in the college precisely because this process has been successful and in order to socialise others (the students or trainees) to the same norms and practices...

It is still the case, therefore, that, as Venables (1967) observes, the technical teacher appears to see him or herself chiefly as the engineer, the secretary, the welder, the fashion designer or the surveyor who happens to be teaching. The staff in such departments do not (either collectively or individually) consistently see themselves as educators...

This is the key to the culture of the FE college – the success of a first occupational socialisation process (without which the teacher would not obtain the FE job) combined with the lack of opportunity and incentive to develop another vocational identity (that of the professional teacher) alongside the first, as well as the potential for conflict between the two. As indicated, this creates further obstacles to the FE professional project, as well as disunity and disagreement (about such things as organisational goals, for example) within the wider professional group...

Conclusion: the professional FE teacher?

Browning (1997) notes that to link the words 'professional' and 'teacher' in the current political climate could be interpreted as a subversive act and to add 'FE' in this context offers, she says, a bold challenge to many people's perceptions. This article has attempted to account (at least in part) for these perceptions of the FE teacher and to explore some of the factors underlying the current crisis. It has been argued that the teaching profession in FE is, indeed, fragmented and on the defensive, and that the reasons for this relate to its history and to its structure, to its marginal status in the education system as a whole and to official and political neglect.

Its culture is 'thin'; uncertain of the nature or value of a shared body of professional knowledge, unable to require all entrants to qualify formally as teachers (and therefore to acquire such knowledge), compelled to accept recruits into its ranks from hugely diverse backgrounds and entry routes, with no means of controlling their numbers, the professional group lacks closure and is struggling to develop any sense of its collective status or identity. With the nature of their work influenced and controlled to such a large extent from the margins, by central agencies and by external forces, with the erosion and weakening of such professional boundaries as have existed (as between 'teacher' and 'librarians', for example) and with growing financial constraints and pressures (resulting in, for instance, increased numbers of part-time employees), the low status of the profession is unarguable. In addition, the diverse cultures within the FE college have few strong common bonds and a real need to retain previous occupational allegiances (to ensure credibility as vocational teachers). The structure and organisation of most colleges does little to create opportunity or incentive for developing another identity (that of the FE teacher) and there is often disunity and disagreement (about organisational goals, for instance) within the wider professional group. The existence of dual professional identities amongst many of its staff should be a source of strength, both for the individual and for the sector as a whole, but the official failure to support the development of a full professional identity for the FE teacher, the prioritising (both officially and unofficially) of the first occupational identity, at the expense of the second, has resulted in anomaly and confusion. Add to this the growth of a new culture of managerialism, with its emphasis on the individual, on 'performance management', on accountability within hierarchies, and the likelihood is that the profession will find it difficult to act collectively, that its professional project will continue to be undermined and that change will be slow to come...

References

Ainley P & Bailey B (1997) *The business of learning* Cassell
Board of Education (1944) *Teachers and youth leaders: McNair report* HMSO

Browning S (1997) Book review of 'The professional FE teacher' by J Robson (ed) (Avebury: Ashgate Publishing) *Journal of Vocational Education and Training* 49 (1), pp171–174

Cantor WM & Roberts IF (1986) *Further education in England and Wales* 3rd edn Routledge & Kegan Paul

Department for Education & Employment (DfEE) (1997) *Higher education in the learning society: the Dearing report* HMSO

Department of Education & Science/Department of Employment (DES/DOE) (1985) *White Paper: Education & training for young people Cmnd 9482* HMSO

Further and Higher Education Act (1992) HMSO

Further Education Funding Council (1997) *Quality and standards in FE: Chief Inspector's report* FEFC

Macdonald K (1995) *The sociology of the professions* Sage

Stanton G (1989) 'The Further Education (FE) mainstream and open learning' in N Paine (ed) *Open learning in transition: an agenda for action* Kogan Page

UNESCO (1973) *Technical and vocational teacher education and training* UNESCO

Venables E (1967) *The young worker at college: a study of a local tech* Faber & Faber

Ware J (1996) 'Flexible learning in FE and the implications for teachers' in J Robson (ed) *The professional FE teacher* Avebury

Young M, Lucas N, Sharp C & Cunningham B (1995) *Teacher education for the further education sector: training the lecturer of the future* AFC/Institute of Education

3.   Becoming a Professional Teacher

Liz Beaty

Introduction

No matter how expert in your discipline or profession you are, teaching can still be a daunting prospect. You might ask yourself: Will the students learn? What are their needs and how do I meet them? You may also have more personal worries: Will they like me? What should I wear? Should I try to get close to them or should I be aloof and distant? Teaching ... takes many forms, and the answers to these questions will inevitably be ones that you must answer for yourself. They will, of course, also be formed by the context of the department and colleagues with whom you work. Fundamentally, however, developing as a teacher will require you to focus on learning from your own experience through reflection illuminated by educational theory and the informed planning of improvements...

The nature of professional development

The term 'professional' describes an attitude to work and not merely a type of job. To take a professional approach means acting in a professional way. It involves an approach to life and work which includes taking responsibility, being creative and critically questioning our own individual practice.

Developing your own professional approach goes beyond knowledge and skills to the core of personal growth and the ability to harness this growth into more effective action. Furthermore, it acknowledges that this development is never complete, there is always more to learn about yourself, your students and the complexity of the world in which we live.

Professional practice requires the development of insight and wisdom in responding to idiosyncrasies of the situations that face us. Professional development, therefore, crucially involves learning from experience. There is always a mixture of the expected and the novel in any situation. The teacher faces a blend of known personalities and the unique interplay between them. The challenge for the professional is to learn from experience in a way which does not destroy the fresh interest offered by each particular event or activity.

We learn from experience through a process of observation, reflection and generalisation and by recognising patterns within the complexity of our experience. We also learn to tailor our actions by reference to our own internal store of experience which allows us to say 'I have seen a situation similar to this before'. We learn to recognise emergent events so that they no longer take us by surprise. On the whole we do all of this naturally, without deliberate processes of record keeping. We may also build up knowledge of our own individual habits, styles and tendencies.

We learn to distinguish events that will challenge us from ones where we are comfortable and at ease. This store of self knowledge is also fundamental to the development of professional practice.

Professional development and reflective practice

A useful model of professional development can be based on a view of skill acquisition from novice to expert. In this model, skill is acquired through routine practice and decision making. Thus, for the novice, experiential knowledge is small and decisions will be tentative and rule bound to avoid mistakes. After some experience the application of rules becomes more automatic and there are fewer surprises in practice. Thus longer-term goals become visible and procedures are applied routinely and with less anxiety. The expert moves beyond rules to more 'intuitive' action where a deep understanding of context informs a view of what is routine and what is novel. This model demonstrates the importance of rules in the early stages of professional development but also the crucial nature of learning from experience. In the early days of our professional practice, the experience we use to help us make decisions is limited and we need more guidance. Through reflecting on our teaching we learn to discriminate between features of the environment that are important to the learning outcomes and those which are less so. We learn to be guided by our tacit knowledge and perception of patterns.

Reflective practice is important to the development of all professionals because it enables us to learn from experience. Although, as we all learn from experience, more and more experience does not guarantee more and more learning. Twenty years of teaching may not equate to 20 years of learning about teaching but may be only one year repeated 20 times. This repeated experience may even result in some inefficient or ineffective habits which will be very difficult to change.

Our normal human reactions to events ensure that we think a great deal about things when they are novel; we are keen to find patterns which help us to understand the new situation. We are also more likely to think through situations when they have caused us pain. We search for a cause that will help us to act differently in the future to avoid the pain. Over time, however, the same experience repeated will have less impact on us and we form habits that are very difficult to change. Most of our teaching experience is neither particularly novel nor painful. There are, therefore, many times when our normal reactions to events are insufficient in themselves to encourage reflection. We should not rely solely on our natural process of reflecting on experience, but actively seek ways to ensure that reflection itself becomes a habit, ensuring our continuing development as a professional teacher...

The use of observation, feedback and dialogue

The teacher is essentially a human being and learning is a core activity throughout life. For some development to occur, we first have to discover what it is that we do not know.

There are, therefore, new things to be learnt from reflection with the aid of other people. For professional teachers, the most immediate benefit can come from using various forms of feedback from students to encourage reflection. Their perspectives, attitudes, responses and feelings provide rich data for reflection on our professional practice. Moreover, they focus our attention in a helpful way on the result of our work. Finding ways to access the student perspective is crucial to our professional development as teachers. It is also important to view this seeking of feedback as a core process throughout the teaching and learning interaction and not simply something to be done at the very end of a course. After all, it is only during the course that we can influence the student's experience. Afterwards it is too late to discover, for example, that we were moving too fast or too slowly, and the next group of students may react differently...

Colleagues can also be very helpful in aiding our reflection. They are likely to be able to empathise with us and we can trust their professional ability to maintain confidentiality. More experienced colleagues can use their knowledge and insight to illuminate reflections on our own practice. Unlike students, they may notice our actions from the point of view of a professional. They will also be able to imagine reactions to our suggested changes for the future. A colleague's knowledge of the discipline can be an important focus for this reflection. On the other hand, a peer who is not in the same subject area could focus more on professional processes rather than on the content of our teaching. The support of peers provides an opportunity for learning beyond that of private reflection by the individual. It also emphasises a view of teaching as a team activity. Students rely on many lecturers and other staff for their learning and it is therefore important that we work together with our colleagues to facilitate that learning.

While discussions do help us to reflect on our practice, rarely does a general discussion allow us to interrogate in a specific and deep way our own personal approaches. It is easy to have a discussion about teaching and learning, for example, without feeling that there are any conclusions to be drawn about our own approach as a teacher. The concentrated and intentional process of deliberately reflecting with the aid of peers is an altogether more potent tool for professional development. Finding ways to focus dialogue onto your own needs for development is an important way to manage continuing professional development.

The importance of action

Reflection alone is not sufficient for professional development to occur. The real test is developed practice. Reflection then is a middle ground where theories are brought to bear on the analysis of past action; the really important stage comes after this and could be thought of as planning. To assess the significance of learning from experience we need to ask 'So what'?

After any period of reflection on practice should come planned change. Changing practice might be as simple as using a larger font on an overhead transparency or it might be as difficult as being more assertive with ground rules in seminars. We can alter some things just by making an individual decision to do so while other changes require discussion and decisions with colleagues. Development is rarely simple. It may require some deliberate knowledge or skill enhancement and it often requires a team approach, but action is the important key to making a difference to our professional practice. Just knowing we could improve, even identifying how this could be achieved, is not enough. We need to take steps towards developing our capabilities and improving our working environment.

The crucial question, therefore, is: What next? We need to plan in two ways. Firstly, we need to plan to meet our own identified development needs. Reflection can help us to identify a need but reflection by itself does not deliver the development. From the identification of a need, we may require further targeted training or greater theoretical knowledge. We may be able to undertake this for ourselves or we may need the help of a mentor or educational development specialist.

Secondly, we need to plan for future practice. This again may be an individual activity but will more likely require a team approach and a series of experimental changes. Change is unlikely to be 'right first time' and therefore will require evaluation and modifications. Thus development becomes cyclical, a constant round of evaluation and development of practice both on yourself as a professional and on the activities that you perform in your professional practice.

Continuing professional development

A professional approach involves acknowledgement of our own limitations and a willingness to involve others or to take particular care with aspects of the work where we are less able. Newly appointed professionals may be more aware of the build-up of this experience than someone who is very experienced. After some time, however, our ability to learn something new every day tends to diminish. We may stop feeling like a learner and rely solely on our current skills and knowledge. It is at these times when the support and challenge of peers is crucial to professional development.

Most of us experience a degree of isolation in our work. It is not so much that we work alone, more that we have few opportunities to reflect with others on our own practice. We can notice how other people work, but we are unlikely to discuss differences unless they actively interfere with our own way of doing things. This can bring complacency and an increasing resistance to change. We may need to invest time in supporting our own development in a more formal way.

Continuing professional development requires both support and challenge. It demands that we keep on learning and that we inform our learning through reflection on practice and by managing our staff development. It is therefore important that we monitor our needs and take opportunities for education and training.

The Institute of Personnel and Development (IPD) has set out the following guiding principles ...

- *Development should be continuous, in the sense that the professional should always be actively seeking improved performance.*
- *Development should be owned and managed by the individual learner.*

- *Development should start from the individual's current learning state, while fitting appropriate organisation or client needs.*
- *Learning objectives should be clear although they may be complex, and wherever possible should meet the needs of the organisation as well as the individual.*
- *Investment of time in learning should be regarded as being as important as investment in any other activity.*

These principles emphasise the need to be accountable in what we do for our development of practice. In teaching, the needs of the student, the [institution] and the wider society have a bearing on the way we approach our professional development.

4. Ethical Principles in University Teaching

Liz Beaty

Preamble

The purpose of this document is to provide a set of basic ethical principles that define the professional responsibilities of university [lecturers] in their role as teachers.

Ethical principles are conceptualized here as general guidelines, ideals or expectations that need to be taken into account, along with other relevant conditions and circumstances, in the design and analysis of university teaching.

The intent of this document is not to provide a list of ironclad rules, or a systematic code of conduct, along with prescribed penalties for infractions, that will automatically apply in all situations and govern all eventualities. Similarly, the intent is not to contradict the concept of academic freedom, but rather to describe ways in which academic freedom can be exercised in a responsible manner...

Principle 1: Content competence

A university teacher maintains a high level of subject matter knowledge and ensures that course content is current, accurate, representative, and appropriate to the position of the course within the student's program of studies.

This principle means that a teacher is responsible for maintaining (or acquiring) subject matter competence not only in areas of personal interest but in all areas relevant to course goals or objectives. Appropriateness of course content implies that what is actually taught in the course is consistent with stated course objectives... Achievement of content competence requires that the teacher take active steps to be up-to-date in content areas relevant to his or her courses...

Specific examples of failure to fulfil the principle of content competence occur when an instructor teaches subjects for which she or he has an insufficient knowledge base, [or] when an instructor misinterprets research evidence to support a theory or social policy favoured by the instructor...

Principle 2: Pedagogical competence

A pedagogically competent teacher communicates the objectives of the course to students, is aware of alternative instructional methods or strategies, and selects methods of instruction that, according to research evidence (including personal or self-reflective research), are effective in helping students to achieve the course objectives.

This principle implies that, in addition to knowing the subject matter, a teacher has adequate pedagogical knowledge and skills, including communication of objectives, selection of effective instructional methods, provision of practice and feedback opportunities, and accommodation of student diversity. If mastery of a certain skill (e.g. critical analysis, design of experiments) is part of the course objectives and will be considered in evaluation and grading of students, the teacher provides students with adequate opportunity to practice and receive feedback on that skill during the course. If learning styles differ significantly for different students or groups of students, the teacher is aware of these differences and, if feasible, varies her or his style of teaching accordingly.

To maintain pedagogical competence, an instructor takes active steps to stay current regarding teaching strategies that will help students learn relevant knowledge and skills and will provide equal educational opportunity for diverse groups...

Specific examples of failure to fulfil the principle of pedagogical competence include using an instructional method or assessment method that is incongruent with the stated course objectives (e.g. using exams consisting solely of fact-memorisation questions when the main objective of the course is to teach problem solving skills); and failing to give students adequate opportunity to practise or learn skills that are included in the course objectives and will be tested in the final exam.

Principle 3: Dealing with sensitive topics

Topics that students are likely to find sensitive or discomforting are dealt with in an open, honest, and positive way.

Among other things, this principle means that the teacher acknowledges from the outset that a particular topic is sensitive, and explains why it is necessary to include it in the course syllabus. Also, the teacher identifies his or her own perspective on the topic and compares it to alternative approaches or interpretations, thereby providing students with an understanding of the complexity of the issue and the difficulty of achieving a single 'objective' conclusion. Finally, in order to provide a safe and open environment for class discussion, the teacher invites all students to state their position on the issue, sets ground rules for discussion, is respectful of students even when it is necessary to disagree, and encourages students to be respectful of one another...

[An] example of a sensitive topic occurs when a film depicting scenes of child abuse is shown, without forewarning, in a developmental psychology class. Assuming that such a film has a valid pedagogical role, student distress and discomfort can be minimised by warning students in advance of the content of the film.

Principle 4: Student development

The overriding responsibility of the teacher is to contribute to the intellectual development of the student, at least in the context of the teacher's own area of expertise, and to avoid actions such as exploitation and discrimination that detract from student development.

According to this principle, the teacher's most basic responsibility is to design instruction that facilitates learning and encourages autonomy and independent thinking in students, to treat students with respect and dignity, and to avoid actions that detract unjustifiably from student development. Failure to take responsibility for student development occurs when a teacher comes to class under-prepared, fails to design effective instruction, coerces students to adopt a particular value or point of view, or fails to discuss alternative theoretical interpretations...

Less obvious examples of failure to take responsibility for student development can arise when teachers ignore the power differential between themselves and students and behave in ways that exploit or denigrate students. Such behaviours include sexual or racial discrimination, or derogatory comments toward students...

In some cases, the teacher's responsibility to contribute to student development can come into conflict with responsibilities to other agencies, such as the university, the academic discipline, or society as a whole... There are no hard and fast rules that govern situations such as these. The teacher must weigh all conflicting responsibilities, possibly consult with other individuals, and come to a reasoned decision.

Principle 5: Dual relationships with students

To avoid conflict of interest, a teacher does not enter into dual-role relationships with students that are likely to detract from student development or lead to actual or perceived favouritism on the part of the teacher.

This principle means that it is the responsibility of the teacher to keep relationships with students focused on pedagogical goals and academic requirements. The most obvious example of a dual relationship that is likely to impair teacher objectivity and/or detract from student development is any form of sexual or close personal relationship with a current student. Other potentially problematic dual relationships include: accepting a teaching (or grading) role with respect to a member of one's immediate family, a close friend, or an individual who is also a client, patient, or business partner; excessive socialising with students outside of class, either individually or as a group; lending money to or borrowing money from students; giving gifts to or accepting gifts from students... Even if the teacher believes that she or he is maintaining objectivity in situations such as these, the perception of favouritism on the part of other students is as educationally disastrous as actual favouritism or unfairness.

If a teacher does become involved in a dual relationship with a student, despite efforts to the contrary, it is the responsibility of the teacher to notify his or her supervisor of the situation as soon as possible, so that alternative arrangements can be made for supervision or evaluation of the student. Although there are definite pedagogical benefits to establishing good rapport with students and interacting with students both inside and outside the classroom, there are also serious risks of exploitation, compromise of academic standards, and harm to student development. It is the responsibility of the teacher to prevent these risks from materialising into real or perceived conflicts of interest.

Principle 6: Confidentiality

Student grades, attendance records, and private communications are treated as confidential materials, and are released only with student consent, or for legitimate academic purposes, or if there are reasonable grounds for believing that releasing such information will be beneficial to the student or will prevent harm to others.

This principle suggests that students are entitled to the same level of confidentiality in their relationships with teachers as would exist in a lawyer-client or doctor-patient relationship. Violation of confidentiality in the teacher-student relationship can cause students to distrust teachers and to show decreased academic motivation. Whatever rules or policies are followed with respect to confidentiality of student records, these should be disclosed in full to students at the beginning of the academic term.

In the absence of adequate grounds (i.e. student consent, legitimate purpose, or benefit to student) any of the following could be construed as a violation of confidentiality: providing student academic records to a potential employer, or researcher, or private investigator, or discussing a student's grades or academic problems with another faculty member...

Principle 7: Respect for colleagues

A university teacher respects the dignity of her or his colleagues and works co-operatively with colleagues in the interest of fostering student development.

This principle means that in interactions among colleagues with respect to teaching, the overriding concern is the development of students. Disagreements between colleagues relating to teaching are settled privately, if possible, with no harm to student development. If a teacher suspects that a colleague has shown incompetence or ethical violations in teaching, the teacher takes responsibility for investigating the matter thoroughly and consulting privately with the colleague before taking further action.

A specific example of failure to show respect for colleagues occurs when a teacher makes unwarranted derogatory comments in the classroom about the competence of another teacher...

Principle 8: Valid assessment of students

Given the importance of assessment of student performance in university teaching and in students' lives and careers, instructors are responsible for taking adequate steps to ensure that assessment of students is valid, open, fair and congruent with course objectives.

This principle means that the teacher is aware of research (including personal or self-reflective research) on the advantages and disadvantages of alternative methods of assessment, and based on this knowledge the teacher selects assessment techniques that are consistent with the objectives of the course and at the same time are as reliable and valid as possible. Furthermore, assessment procedures and grading standards are communicated clearly to students at the beginning of the course, and except in rare circumstances there is no deviation from the announced procedures.

Student exams, papers, and assignments are graded carefully and fairly through the use of a rational marking system that can be communicated to students. By means appropriate for the size of the class, students are provided with prompt and accurate feedback on their performance at regular intervals throughout the course, plus an explanation as to how their work was graded, and constructive suggestions as to how to improve their standing in the course. In a similar vein, teachers are fair and objective in writing letters of reference for students.

One example of an ethically questionable assessment practice is to grade students on skills that were not part of the announced course objectives and/or were not allocated adequate practice opportunity during the course...

Principle 9: Respect for institution

In the interests of student development, a university teacher is aware of and respects the educational goals, policies, and standards of the institution in which he or she teaches.

This principle implies that a teacher shares a collective responsibility to work for the good of the university as a whole, to uphold the educational goals and standards of the university, and to abide by university policies and regulations pertaining to the education of students.

Specific examples of failure to uphold the principle of respect for the institution include engaging in excessive work activity outside the university that conflicts with university teaching responsibilities; and being unaware of or ignoring valid university regulations on provision of course outlines, scheduling of exams, or academic misconduct.

Part Two – Professional Development

In her discussion of the nature of professional development, Liz Beaty (page 17) has described how we 'learn from experience through a process of observation, reflection and generalisation, and by recognising patterns within the complexity of our own experience'. This deliberate activity of development, she says later, 'becomes cyclical, a constant round of evaluation and development of practice' (page 20).

The purpose of Part Two is to explore this cyclical process in more detail, and to present a number of practical guidelines to action. Lynda Hall examines the concept and practice of self-assessment and outlines the central role that the observation of teaching (both observing and being observed) and the sharing of feedback can play in providing the important information on which to base the process of analysis and reflection. She emphasises the need for planned action to arise from this reflection, so that learning from experience does lead to changes in everyday practice and to the extension and refinement of teaching skills.

For both the observer and the observed to benefit from the experience, however, an observation needs to be carefully planned. In the next extract Hazel Fullerton provides guidance for all participants before, during and after the event.

If the process of reflection is to be made public and shared with others (for whatever purposes) then we meet the problem of becoming familiar with the appropriate language for the production of documents and the presentation of those conceptual frameworks which will allow us to articulate our analysis and reflection. Christine Butterworth, in the third contribution, considers the nature of reflective writing, and the way in which theoretical perspectives can be incorporated into such writing.

The final extract in this Part is from a paper by Kathryn Ecclestone, which examines the different interpretations of 'reflection' present in training and development work with PCET practitioners. Her overall concern in the paper is to critique the spread of competence-based programmes of initial or in-service training for post-compulsory teachers, and the way in which such programmes claim to incorporate 'reflection' or 'reflective practice' into their lists of competences. She argues that there is currently an unhelpful confusion of possible meanings for these terms, and that PCET teacher educators should clarify their different interpretations of 'reflection', since there is a danger that the proliferation of competence-based training for teachers and trainers in the post-16 sector will mean that only one type of 'reflection' will prevail.

5.   Learning from Experience

Lynda Hall

Introduction

The process of professional development throughout a career is conventionally described in terms of a continuous cycle of reflection on experience, leading to the planning and implementation of change:

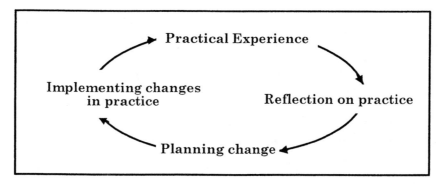

Figure 1   The process of continuing professional development

But within this larger cycle another day-to-day cycle is taking place which is just as important and usually much more immediate. This cycle should be familiar to all teachers, and goes on as a routine part of the deliberate planning and evaluation of our teaching:

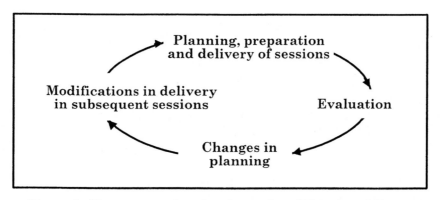

Figure 2   The process of evaluating and modifying teaching

It is difficult enough to make time in this daily round to think deeply about our experiences or to bring educational theories to bear on the analysis of past action. Yet, although a thorough and detailed analysis may need to wait until a later date, we can think about and record our experiences, identify problems and work out

31

solutions to them as we go along. We can also gather information about our own practice from being observed by others and we can learn from the experience of observing our colleagues. The material so gathered should provide a rich store of information for subsequent analysis and reflection.

This section, then, is concerned with the day-to-day teaching and training cycle, of which self-assessment and evaluation, the observation of one's peers and the exchange of feedback, form important parts.

Self-assessment and evaluation

Teachers today have less freedom than in the past. Over the last few years there has been increased monitoring of the work of teachers through inspections and staff appraisal and the demands of institutional quality assurance systems. Nevertheless, teachers still have a fair amount of autonomy. They are largely free to determine how they teach and, to a lesser extent, what they teach. This freedom places a responsibility upon teachers to monitor their own professional standards and to review their practice regularly.

Self-assessment involves looking critically at what we do and how we are performing, with the aim of improving our teaching and thus the learning of our students. Although self-assessment often identifies weaknesses or problem areas which need to be addressed, it is not necessarily 'critical' in that sense, and can also help us to identify the strengths which can be built upon. For self-assessment to be useful, it needs to be carried out regularly and systematically, soon after a teaching session has taken place. If we only think about our performance after sessions which go wrong then we will focus on the negatives and fail to recognise the positive aspects of our work. Similarly if self-assessment only involves self-congratulation when things go well then weaknesses will remain and may harden into bad habits which are difficult to break.

The benefits of self-assessment

Although it requires some effort and commitment, many benefits can be gained from regular self-assessment. These include:

1. *Increased self-confidence and personal satisfaction*
   Self-assessment is not synonymous with self-criticism. Noting what we do well, identifying our strengths and recognising where we have improved increases self-confidence and engenders feelings of satisfaction. This in turn may motivate us to work harder at overcoming weaknesses or provide the impetus to experiment and try out new ideas.

2. *Greater understanding of the teaching and learning process*
   During the process of looking critically at what we do and trying to explain to ourselves (and to others) why things have worked or not worked, we are developing and refining our own theories about teaching, learning, student behaviour, group dynamics and so on. The process may lead us to make new connections, have fresh insights, clarify our thinking or review our assumptions. This new learning can then be applied in the classroom.

3. *Improved student learning and better relationships with students*
The main beneficiaries of a critical approach to teaching and learning will be the students. An effective and productive learning experience for students is likely to increase their motivation and reduce classroom management problems.

4. *Increased self-knowledge and awareness*
The way we teach reflects our background, experiences, beliefs and values. Teachers can't divorce themselves from their own backgrounds or from the context in which they teach. It is easy not to notice things when we are not looking for them. Recording and examining the events that take place during a session and how we acted or reacted should heighten awareness of our values, beliefs and prejudices, thus increasing self-knowledge.

5. *Identification of areas for further professional development*
Evaluating our practice over a period of time often reveals the need for some new learning. This may be learning new skills or acquiring more knowledge. It provides data for action research and reflective practice.

Getting started

If the benefits of self-assessment are to be realised then thinking must be followed by action, and action by thinking. Figure 3 illustrates well the processes involved in self-assessment and the link between thinking and action.

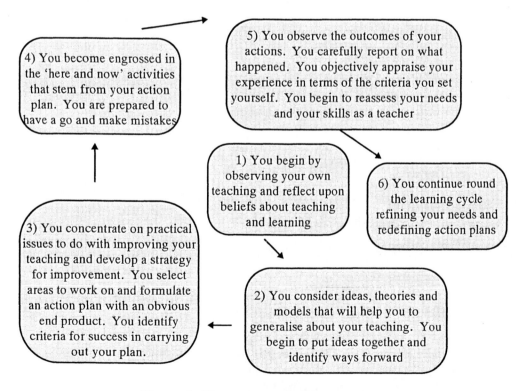

Figure 3   The process of self-assessment

(Gibbs, 1988: 104)

33

Initially it may be useful to look at all aspects of the teaching and learning process. The main areas to review are:

- planning and preparation – the structuring of subject matter, the selection of teaching methods, the preparation of student activities and learning resources
- performance or delivery – how well the plan has been put into action or has worked in practice
- relationships with students, and student learning.

But this may not always be the most productive way forward. An alternative to the broad review is to focus upon particular aspects of practice, for example planning or classroom management or question and answer techniques. One technique for reviewing current performance and identifying areas for development, known as SWAIN (Strengths, Weaknesses, Aspirations, Interests, Needs), is shown in Annex B3 to this section (pages 46–7). A SWAIN analysis could well provide a useful starting point for self-assessment.

Whatever the starting point, it is important that thoughts and feelings are written down soon after the event. Memories fade and details can be difficult to recall accurately after a day or so. With the passage of time it is possible to persuade ourselves that things were neither as good or as bad as they seemed in the classroom. This might well be true but a more objective assessment can be made on the basis of recorded facts rather than faded memories. You may be able to arrange to record some sessions either on video or audio tape. This makes it possible to evaluate actual performance rather than recollections of it.

Having reviewed and thought about a session, the next step, as indicated in Figure 3, is to identify areas to work upon and to set clear objectives for improvement. This could involve drawing up an Action Plan along the lines suggested below.

Action plan

- identify and select areas for improvement
- plan how to improve
- carry out the plan
- observe and record the effects of action
- think about these effects, decide on future action.

Self-assessment techniques

There are a number of techniques which can aid self-assessment and evaluation. These can be broadly divided into two types:

1. Checklists and self-evaluation questionnaires

These usually consist of a fairly lengthy list of questions or statements which invite teachers either to rate their performance or to provide short answers, often just yes or no. They tend to cover many aspects of teaching and can be useful for jogging the memory and helping to identify strengths and weaknesses. Some questionnaires contain more open-ended questions which encourage teachers to identify their own lists of strengths and weaknesses. Although they may be a useful starting point, checklists and questionnaires are not enough on their own. Their main weakness is that they do not explicitly encourage teachers to think about and explain what actually happened during a session. Examples of checklists and self-evaluation questionnaires can be found in Annexes A1 – A4.

2. *Structured self-evaluation forms*

More useful for encouraging open-ended self-assessment is a proforma that uses several headings. The headings can be chosen with one of a number of purposes in mind, for example:

- to help structure and organise recollections
- to focus attention on particular aspects of a session
- to aid the process of remembering, identifying and analysing strengths and weaknesses.

Teachers can prepare their own evaluation forms and change them to suit their individual purposes. Examples can be found in Annexes B1 – B3.

Peer observation

Usually when somebody else observes our teaching the main purpose is to make a judgement about our competence. This is the case when university tutors observe student teachers or line managers or inspectors observe practising teachers. But the main purpose of observation by a colleague or peer is to provide feedback which can be used to identify areas for improvement or development. This is not a substitute for self-assessment but another source of information to supplement experience.

Benefits of observation

There are a number of benefits to be gained both from being observed by and observing a peer. In both instances the discussion after the event is of crucial importance. The benefits may include:

1. *Increased self-confidence*

Observing a peer enables us to compare our skills and the way we work with others, an opportunity all too rare in teaching. We may find that our skills compare very favourably or that we are not doing as badly as we thought, with a consequent increase in our confidence. Receiving constructive and supportive feedback from a peer can also increase confidence and motivation.

2. *Greater self-knowledge*

There are some sorts of information about our performance which are difficult to gather whilst we are engaged in the teaching and learning process. An observer can feed back to us aspects of our behaviour which would otherwise remain hidden. For example, we may be unaware that we are giving more time and attention to some students rather than to others. An observer can also provide us with some insight into how the students may be experiencing our teaching.

3. *The opportunity to discuss experiences with a supportive colleague*

Teachers can sometimes feel isolated in their own classroom especially if they are experiencing problems. It is often difficult to share these experiences with others who have no firsthand knowledge of the issue. Discussing a problem with someone who has observed the situation may help in the search for a solution.

4. *The opportunity to learn from others*

As mentioned already, we generally work alone in the classroom and do not often have the opportunity to see other practitioners at work. Observing others may provide us with new ideas about how to manage the learning group, teach a particular concept, motivate students and so on. Discussing and analysing a session with an observer may provide fresh insights and new tools for analysis.

Giving and receiving feedback

Feedback can be enormously helpful but it is neither easy to give nor to receive. Some people find it difficult to say 'you did that well' and even more people find it difficult to say 'you did that badly'. It can be difficult to listen to and accept feedback. Some people have a tendency to hear only the negative points and not the positives; others become defensive when they think they are being criticised. So, the way in which feedback is given is important. Handled carefully and sensitively it can be a constructive and rewarding experience for both parties.

Giving feedback

1. Give feedback as soon as possible after the event and make sure that it remains confidential.

2. Give the recipient the opportunity to express his/her feelings and thoughts first, before you give feedback. Encourage them to identify problems and suggest solutions. If necessary ask questions to help them think through the issues.

3. Give feedback on the behaviour you observed rather than about the person. Be specific and focus on behaviour which can be changed. Remember that the purpose of the feedback is to help the other person improve their teaching.

4. Give positive feedback first so that the listener is more likely to be receptive to any negative feedback. But remember that just giving positive feedback is not going to help the recipient to improve and just giving negative feedback is likely to have a demoralising effect. Follow negative points with a discussion about what can be done to improve.

5. Don't try to give feedback on everything you observed. Select the most important aspects to discuss and be clear about what you want to say. Nobody can concentrate on changing everything at once so if you try to cover too much the recipient is likely to stop listening.

Receiving feedback

1. Listen carefully to the feedback without interrupting to explain your actions. But ask questions if the feedback is unclear or you need more information.

2. Avoid becoming defensive. Assume that the feedback is intended to help you improve your performance.

3. Think about how you can make use of the feedback to improve your teaching.

Assessment

The practice of teaching is also from time to time subject to observation by a third party for the purpose of assessment. Teachers and trainers are accountable for the quality of their teaching to their employing institutions, to examining and funding bodies, not to mention the universities and colleges which award teacher training qualifications.

Though the purpose of observation in this case may be summative rather than formative, we should not expect the procedures to be very different from those we have outlined here.

References

Gibbs G (1988) *Learning by doing: a guide to teaching and learning methods* Further Education Unit

Gibbs G, Habeshaw S & Habeshaw T (1988) *53 ways to appraise your teaching* Technical and Educational Services

O'Neill M & Pennington G (1992) 'Evaluating teaching and courses from an active learning perspective, Part 1' in *Effective learning and teaching in higher education* CVCP Universities' Staff Development and Training Unit

Self-evaluation questionnaire 1

The following questions can be used to evaluate your planning and performance. They are not intended to be an exhaustive list but may provide some useful starting points for self-assessment.

Preparation

Were the learning outcomes clear? Were they appropriate?

What activities/strategies were incorporated? Were these varied?

Was there a logical, developmental sequence? Did this allow for variation among students?

Were suitable materials and resources prepared and used?

Was there a summary of the lesson?

Performance

Was the session introduced effectively?

Were the pace and level appropriate?

Was the manner of presentation (voice, language, aids) suitable?

Were various teaching methods used effectively?

Were students involved in learning?

Was adaptability shown? Were unplanned incidents used to good effect?

Were there any major departures from the plan? Why?

Relationships

Was there a co-operative atmosphere – conducive to learning?

Was respect for all individuals shown – and expected?

Was psychological safety ensured? Were student contributions valued?

Assessment

Were learning checks made – relevant to outcomes?

Were they appropriately timed?

Was the progress of the session related to the students' responses?

Did learning take place?

Annex A2

Self-evaluation questionnaire 2

This is a very much more open-ended set of questions.

When I ran this session, what seemed to go well was...

And what didn't seem to go as well as I had hoped was...

The next time I run this session:

I will avoid:

I will change:

I will include:

(from O'Neill & Pennington, 1992)

Annex A3

Checklist

Record with a tick in the appropriate column the comments which come closest to your opinion of your own performance in each of the following areas

	How well did I...?	very well	well	not very well	poorly
1	link this session to other sessions				
2	introduce this session				
3	make the learning outcomes clear to the students				
4	move clearly from stage to stage				
5	emphasise key points				
6	summarise the session				
7	maintain an appropriate pace				
8	capture & maintain student interest				
9	handle problems of inattention				
10	ask questions				
11	handle student questions & responses				
12	plan & direct student tasks				
13	monitor student activity				
14	cope with the range of ability/age				
15	use learning resources				
16	make contact with all class members				
17	cope with individual difficulties				
18	keep the material relevant				
19	use my voice				
20	check on student learning				
21	motivate students				
22	convey my enthusiasm				
23	provide a model of good practice				

(adapted from Gibbs *et al.* 1988)

Annex A4

Checklist and self-evaluation questionnaire

1) How satisfied are you *(Tick **one** column for each item)*	Totally	Fairly	Not very	Not at all
• that the learning tasks were made explicit to your students?				
• that you promoted and maintained your students' interest throughout the session?				
• that you promoted and maintained your students' attention throughout the session?				
• with the way you used questioning techniques?				
• with how you paced the session?				

• with how you:
    introduced the material?
    developed the material?
    consolidated the material?				

• with your use of demonstrations and/or teaching aids?				

• with your success in promoting learning in:
    the weakest student in the class?
    the average students in the class?				

• that the method(s) you adopted was the best way of teaching the topic?				

Continued...

2) List the three most difficult teaching points that occurred in the session. Speculate on the reasons.

3) List the three things you would consider doing differently next time you taught the topic. Write down your reasons.

4) List the three most successful elements in the session. Write down what you consider to be the reasons for their success.

5) Write down your overall impression of your success in teaching this topic on this occasion.

(adapted from O'Neil & Pennington, 1992)

Annex B1

Structured self evaluation form 1

Reflections on your own teaching

After teaching a lesson, write a short account of what took place. Do this as soon as possible after the end of the lesson.

(At this stage don't attempt to evaluate the lesson or your teaching performance; concentrate instead on what actually happened.)

Now try to categorise your observations. Use the following headings:

- Things I did before and during the lesson which should have helped students to learn:

- Any unplanned things I did during the lesson which should have helped my students to learn:

Finally, write a brief statement of this work, describing:

What insights, if any, I gained into the ways in which I helped my students to learn.

(from Gibbs, 1988)

Annex B2

Structured self-evaluation form 2

Describe – what happened in the lesson

Identify – strengths and weaknesses, problem areas, key events

Analyse – the events/issues identified, explain why some things worked and others didn't

Act – what to do in future lessons, solutions to problems, strategies for development

Annex B3

SWAIN: A self-evaluation technique

A 'SWAIN' analysis is similar to a SWOT analysis. It is technique that allows teachers/trainers to identify their personal development needs after an identification and evaluation of their Strengths, Weaknesses, Aspirations and Interests. On the basis of this self-evaluation a plan for improving practice can be drawn up.

Key to the meaning of SWAIN

Strengths:

These are tasks and responsibilities I carry out well (or could do if given the chance!). Questions for reflection:

- should I consolidate my strengths?
- capitalise upon them?
- extend them?
- move beyond them?

Weaknesses:

These are tasks and responsibilities I carry out less well (or try to avoid/postpone). Questions for reflection:

- should I try to develop my skills in these areas?
- should I seek to avoid such tasks or situations in the future?

Aspirations:

These are things I want to be good at or to achieve in the future. Questions for reflection:

- what new tasks/responsibilities do I want to take on?
- what knowledge, understanding, skills, attitudes do I need to acquire or develop to prepare for such new responsibilities?

Interests:

These are tasks I enjoy or am inherently motivated to undertake. Questions for reflection:

- what are my main interests in my present job/role?
- what other interests have I that are not currently fulfilled?

Needs

Now, in the light of the above, make a summary of those areas or aspects of your work which you believe should be developed further. Put these in order of priority and determine a personal time-scale for engagement with them.

Use the proforma below for your analysis, or design your own.

Task	Strengths	Weaknesses	Aspirations	Interests	Needs

(adapted from O'Neil & Pennington, 1992)

6. Guidelines for the Observation of Teaching

Hazel Fullerton

1. Before the observation

Selecting the observer

It is crucial that the observer is known to, and respected by, the person being observed. There should be a professional and trusting relationship between the two for the observation process to provide maximum benefit to both...

Deciding upon what session to observe

It is best to decide which session(s) is to be observed in discussion between observed and observer...

At first, it is often best to choose a session where the observed is confident, although experience shows that maximum benefit is likely to be gained where something new, difficult or unfamiliar is being tried out.

It is easier to recall detail immediately after the session, so try to select a session when both the observer and the observed are free for the following hour for discussion.

Aim for no more than a one hour observation. This could be a complete lecture, or part of a practical session (say the first and last 30 minutes)...

Deciding upon what is to be done during the observation

There are many ways to observe sessions, ranging from the open and unplanned to use of highly detailed, pre-designed observation schedules. In most cases, somewhere in between is most appropriate...

Observed and observer should spend some time before the session deciding what is to be done. Things to consider include:

- what the observed wants to achieve from the observation
- where the observer should sit, or whether it is appropriate to wander around (in practical sessions it may be valuable to talk with or observe the students)
- when observed and observer will meet to discuss the session
- what documentation needs to be prepared.

2. During the observation

Questions for the observation

The observer and observed should have a number of aspects and questions in mind when discussing and designing the process of observation. These could include:

- Planning the session:
  - how does the plan relate to previous sessions?
  - are there clear aims and objectives?
  - how does the session fit in with the overall programme for the module?
  - are resources (AVA, handouts, tasks) available at the appropriate points?

- Introducing the session to the students:
  - is it clear to the students how this session relates to previous work?
  - does the introduction 'set the scene' for the session, giving students a clear overview of the way it will develop?

- Delivering and developing the plans:
  - is the communication of ideas relevant, clear and coherent?
  - is there opportunity for the students to clarify their understanding?
  - how is this handled?

- What strategies are used to gain attention, to refocus at intervals and to ensure attention is maintained?
  - are the students motivated?
  - are the teaching methods appropriate to the tasks in hand?
  - are there opportunities for the students to think, question and feed back?
  - what modes of delivery are used; is more than one mode used?

- Concluding the session:
  - is the session drawn to a satisfactory conclusion (or an ongoing series of conclusions)?
  - is there a summary of the main ideas or a review of the point reached so far? does the conclusion look forward to the next session?

Observation methods

There are several ways of observing the process and it is useful for the observer and observed to have these in mind at the stage of planning for the observation. The questions above give some indication of the sort of things to record or remember, but observer and observed will probably also wish to add other aspects.

Observation methods could include:

- a chronological record of what happened throughout the session which can provide a rich, if somewhat unfocused, set of points or notes for later discussion
- before or during the session the observer and observed may decide to focus on specific aspects (e.g. strategies for motivating students, use of AVA, teaching strategies used in a workshop or laboratory session)

- a set of random notes or random observations can be made at regular or irregular intervals during the session for later discussion
- the session could be video-recorded for analysis and discussion of techniques used.

A possible model of an observation:

- spend a few minutes making general notes using some of the questions and ideas outlined above
- identify from those points, one or more areas for further specific and detailed observation
- observe those specific aspects more closely, recording/remembering in such a way that it will provide constructive feedback for the observed.

Remember:

- it is generally more productive if the observer observes against the criteria agreed in initial discussions with the observed
- the aim of the observation is to help improve the skills of the observed, therefore quality feedback is essential. (However, it is likely that the observer will also gain some useful ideas!)

3. After the observation

The purpose of discussion and analysis after the observation is to provide an objective but informed view of the session allowing the observed to gain from that independent perspective. However, it will usually also lead to more wide-ranging discussion of approaches to teaching and learning. Ideas and solutions to issues are often generated.

Discussion after the observation

Obviously it's easier to recall detail immediately, so try to select a session when both observer and observed are free for the following hour for discussion (or as soon as possible).

It is useful for the observed to open the discussion with thoughts as to how the session went; what aims and objectives were achieved; what went well and what was disappointing; or to invite the observed to self-assess against the previously agreed criteria.

If the observer has made a chronological set of notes, these help jog memories and raise questions. The observer might leave the observed to read quietly through the notes for 5 minutes and then encourage response to particular points. Alternatively, the observer may take the observed through the notes, inviting comment.

Either way, the observer can help by using prompting questions throughout the discussion, such as:

- What were you trying to achieve at this point?
- How did you feel about this part?
- Could you have achieved that another way?
- What was the student involvement here?
- How could you have got some, or more, interaction going?
- At what stages were the students having to think?
- How does this relate to the students' existing knowledge? Can they see that relationship?
- How can you check if that objective has been achieved?
- Do you need to find ways of improving their motivation on this?
- What were you most pleased about?

A whole range of points will probably arise. It will help if half a dozen or so can be summarised. That may take the form of identifying three things that have gone really well and three to think about or work on for the future and either to adapt existing practice or to attempt an alternative approach. It may be appropriate to discuss a more general identification of good practice. These points should be agreed between the observed and observer.

7.   Reflective Practice

Christine Butterworth

Introduction

This section traces the development of the concept of reflection, which has been part of the literature on professional training and development since the mid-80s. For nearly 20 years this literature has been pre-occupied with two main problems in supporting professional practice: first, the constant and fast-increasing rate of change in both knowledge and working methods that all professionals have to keep pace with in order to stay up-to-date; second, the development of theories of learning which claim to explain how skilful professionals learn from their experience. What links both these problems is that they both accept that initial, 'front end', training, though necessary, is never sufficient — it soon dates, and it does little to ensure that professionals will continue to learn once they are practising on their own.

The concept of reflection has been central to work on both these problems, and is now a common part of professional training and development — so common that its meaning and use is the focus of close scrutiny. In the next few pages we follow the development of thinking about 'reflection', from the concept's first appearance in the work of Donald Schön, to recent discussion about what the different meanings of 'reflection' might be, and how professional learners might make it part of their practice.

The idea of reflection

The concept of the 'reflective practitioner' has been analysed in great detail by Donald Schön, and the following extracts are from the paper in which he first introduced the term (Schön, 1982). He begins by describing a general public loss of confidence in the 'traditional' view of professionals as experts, and he ascribes their failures to the fact that professional training was based on a faulty view of knowledge.

Professionals seemed powerless to relieve the rapidly-shifting 'crises' of the cities, poverty, environmental pollution and energy... Cumulatively, these events created doubts about the adequacy of professional knowledge, with its theories and techniques, to cure the deeper causes of societal distress. [Trainers saw] ... the puzzle of educating managers for judgement and action under conditions of uncertainty... Different schools [of training] held different and conflicting views of the competences to be acquired, the problem to be solved, even of the nature of the professions themselves... There is widespread recognition of the absence or loss of a stable institutional framework of purpose and knowledge within which professionals can live out their roles and confidently exercise their skills... Artistry is not reducible to the exercise of describable routines ... the competences they were beginning to see as central to professional practice had no place in their underlying model of professional knowledge.

Schön called this discredited model of professional knowledge the 'technical-rational' model, based on a positivist view of the connection between scientific findings and reality, i.e. that they could be simply 'applied' to real-life problems. These scientific 'truths' were discovered by researchers, and handed down to the practitioners or 'appliers' (the status differential between theorists and practitioners is significant); Schön wanted to challenge such a view of the practitioner, maintaining that:

> ... often, in the unstable world of practice, where methods and theories developed in one context are unsuited to another, practitioners function as researchers, inventing the techniques and models appropriate to the situation in hand: real-world problems do not come well-formed. They tend to present themselves, on the contrary, as messy, indeterminate, problematic situations... When a practitioner sets a problem, he [sic] ... decides what he will attend to and what he will ignore... Situations ... may be framed in many different ways ... the artistic processes by which practitioners sometimes make sense of unique cases, and the art they sometimes bring to everyday practice, do not meet the prevailing criteria of rigorous practice. Often, when a competent practitioner recognizes in a maze of symptoms the pattern of a disease ... he does something for which he cannot give a complete or even a reasonably accurate description ... display[ing] skills for which [he] cannot describe procedures or rules. By defining rigour only in terms of technical rationality ... we exclude the most important components of competent practice.

Schön then introduces his new model of professional knowledge, one which is based on a different view of the links that individuals make between theory and practice. For this, he invents the phrase 'reflection-in-action'. He explains it in the following way, and describes the stages in the reflective process:

> When we go about the spontaneous, intuitive performance of the actions of everyday life, we show ourselves to be knowledgeable in a special way. Often, we cannot say what we know... It seems right to say that our knowing is _in_ our action. And similarly, the workaday life of the professional practitioner reveals, in its recognitions, judgements and skills, a pattern of tacit knowing-in-action... Examples of intelligence-in-action include acts of recognition and judgement, as well as the exercise of ordinary physical skills... A child who has learned to throw a ball makes immediate judgements of distance which he co-ordinates, tacitly, with the feeling of bodily movement involved in the act of throwing...

> ... Sometimes our knowing-in-action yields surprises. And we often react to the unexpected by a kind of on-the-spot inquiry which I shall call reflection-in-action... The 'moments' of such a process may be described as follows:

> • In the context of the performance of some task, the performer spontaneously initiates a routine of action that produces an unexpected outcome.

> • The performer notices the unexpected result which he construes as a surprise – an error to be corrected, an anomaly to be made sense of, an opportunity to be exploited.

- *Surprise triggers reflection, directed both to the surprising outcome and to the knowing-in-action that led to it. It is as though the performer asked himself, what is this? and at the same time, what understandings and strategies of mine have led me to produce this?*

- *The performer restructures his understanding of the situation – his framing of the problem he has been trying to solve, his picture of what is going on, or the strategy of action he has been employing.*

- *On the basis of this restructuring, he invents a new strategy of action.*

- *He tries out the new action he has invented, running an on-the-spot experiment whose results he interprets, in turn, as a 'solution', an outcome on the whole satisfactory, or else as a new surprise that calls for a new round of reflection and experiment.*

If we stop and think for a moment about Schön's description of these six stages of reflection – you may wish to read the extract again – we might well be able to recall some recent incident (it may be at work, or outside work) when we came across a problem, or a novel situation, which caused us to stop acting intuitively and re-think what we were doing. We might well find that we went through some or all of the six stages.

The list of points above describes Schön's idea of reflection-in-action, i.e. how we think *while* we do our job. Writing up our professional experience demands, in addition, that we look *back* at our actions and evaluate and analyse them in order to write about them: a process Schön calls reflection-on-action.

Is there such a person as the un- or non-reflective professional? According to Schön, as a practitioner builds up experience and a repertoire of successful responses and strategies, their practice becomes increasingly intuitive: 'rich, efficient, tacit and automatic...' There is a negative side to this, however. The individual's outlook may become narrow, repetitive, conservative, increasingly unreflective as it becomes more intuitive:

> *... systems of intuitively knowing are dynamically conservative, actively defended, highly resistant to change...*

> *Many practitioners find little in the world of practice to occasion reflection. For them, uncertainty is a threat: its admission, a sign of weakness... Yet reflection-in-action is not a rare event. There are teachers ... willing to embrace error, accept confusion, and reflect critically on their previously unexamined assumptions.*

So there are many temptations to indulge in unreflective practice – to go by what you already know, to follow old certainties, rather than keeping an open mind and observing everything with a fresh eye. The main purpose of asking teachers on initial and in-service courses to produce written reflective accounts is to encourage them to see their practice with this fresh eye as they discuss issues with mentors, colleagues and fellow students, and as they are exposed to new ideas.

Models of experiential learning

Following Schön's immensely influential statements about professional knowledge, learning theorists set about establishing models which showed how people learned from experience. One of the most significant of these was Kolb's 'learning cycle' (Kolb, 1984), and in an FEU publication called *Learning by Doing*, Graham Gibbs summarises Kolb's work and offers practical suggestions for supporting experiential learning through reflection (Gibbs, 1988).

It is not sufficient simply to have an experience in order to learn. Without reflecting upon this experience it may quickly be forgotten or its learning potential lost. It is from the feelings and thoughts emerging from this reflection that generalisations or concepts can be generated. And it is generalisations which enable new situations to be tackled effectively.

Similarly, if it is intended that behaviour should be changed by learning, it is not sufficient simply to learn new concepts and develop new generalisations. This learning must be tested out in new situations. The learner must make the link between theory and action by planning for that action, carrying it out, and then reflecting upon it, relating what happens back to the theory.

It is not enough just to do, and neither is it enough just to think. Learning from experience must involve links between the doing and the thinking. The four-stage model of learning by doing which is elaborated in Figure 1 below is that of Kolb.

CONCRETE
EXPERIENCE

↗ ↘

ACTIVE   REFLECTIVE
EXPERIMENTATION   OBSERVATION

↖ ↙

ABSTRACT
CONCEPTUALISATION

Figure 1   Kolb's experiential learning cycle

The terms used here as labels for the four stages come from Kolb's Experiential Learning Theory, and placed in this sequence they form the experiential learning cycle. The cycle can be entered by the learner at any point, but its stages must be followed in sequence.

(Gibbs, 1988: 9–10)

Gibbs then suggests an activity in order to try this out: think of any teaching/training session which you have designed or led, and describe the students' learning activities in terms of this experiential learning cycle. According to Gibbs, there are some fundamental features that such a process must have:

1. *Learners are involved in an <u>active exploration of experience</u>. Experience is used to test out ideas and assumptions rather than to obtain practice passively. Practice can be very important but it is greatly enhanced by reflection.*

2. *Learners must selectively <u>reflect on their experience</u> in a critical way, rather than take experience for granted and assume that the experience on its own is sufficient.*

3. *The experience must matter to the learner. Learners must be <u>committed to the process of exploring and learning</u>.*

4. *There must be scope for the learner to exercise some <u>independence from the teacher</u>... The teacher cannot experience what the learner experiences, or reflect for the learner.*

5. *Experiential learning is not haphazard – a crucial feature is the <u>structure</u> devised by the teacher within which learning takes place.*

6. *<u>Openness to experience</u> is necessary for learners to have the evidence upon which to reflect – learners (must) <u>value their own experience</u> and trust themselves to draw conclusions from it.*

7. *Experiential learning involves a <u>cyclical sequence</u> of learning activities.*

(Gibbs, 1988: 14)

The role of theory in reflective writing

Reflective writing, particularly where it will be judged as evidence of the professional learner's development, and possibly assessed, is not an easy form of writing to produce. There needs to be a balance between honest introspection (that is not too personally revealing) and analytical reviewing that shows the development of conceptualisation about the experiences described, and real connections with the theory that supports those experiences.

So reflective writing is a mixture of the personal (written for yourself as the audience, as you think back systematically) and the public (read by other professionals, possibly for assessment purposes). If you think that the assessment aspect will limit your ability to write honestly and spontaneously, then you may want to write first of all just for yourself as the audience, and produce some draft writing that you can select from and edit for the more public version.

Bloor & Butterworth (1996) have explored how reflective writing can be incorporated into a professional portfolio, i.e. a record of experiences and the learning that they produced, which may cover all or part of a training course, or record a professional career. This part of their discussion looks particularly at the role of theory in the written reflection: both the learner's own 'personal theory' and the research-based, published theory which is often introduced into formal (i.e. taught) learning, in this case an initial teacher training course at the University of Greenwich.

Informal evaluation at Greenwich has shown that one of the areas of difficulty in portfolio work is that of incorporating formal theory into reflective writing. Since Schön, learning theorists have written extensively about the distinctive characteristics of experiential learning and there is much current controversy about the role that formal theory should play in such accounts. Usher (in Bright, 1989) distinguishes practitioner, or informal theory, that is created through experience in a particular work context, from formal theory, which is the sort of knowledge and understanding which is usually taught formally on academic and professional courses. Informal theory, Usher argues, is created through practice and is the result of the interaction between the practitioner's experience and the cognitive models s/he uses to structure the interpretation of their experience. The argument is that practitioner theory is legitimate and deserves the status of a discourse in its own right. However, the problem with informal or practitioner theory is that it is privately experienced, frequently intuitive and therefore not known, and is dependent on the context in which it was generated. Jarvis (1994) also points out that it may be essentially conservative and inflexible unless interrupted or challenged by critical incidents which demand reassessment.

One purpose of some portfolios is to provide an opportunity through the reflective accounts for candidates to make their informal theory more explicit. Through reflection, this informal or practitioner theory can be made more thematic and more explicit. This results in what Argyris & Schön (1980) refer to as 'espoused theory'. Candidates need to provide a reflective, articulated account of their practitioner theory in order to generate their espoused theory: this is not an easy task. There are ways of facilitating the documentation of espoused theory. Writing in the first person does in some ways support this process. This can enhance the sense of personal ownership and is consistent with the personal nature of practitioner theory. Portfolio counsellors can also facilitate this process by supporting and providing feedback to the candidate.

When portfolios are assessed for academic credit, critical evaluation of identified practitioner theory using formal theory may be an important requirement. The idea is to encourage the candidate to use formal theory from relevant professional research and literature to review, evaluate and reconsider their practice. This should necessarily involve some elaboration and reorganisation of the person's existing constructions of informal theory.

References

Argyris C & Schön D (1980) Theory in practice: increasing professional effectiveness Jossey Bass

Bright B (ed) (1989) Theory and practice in the study of adult education Routledge

Jarvis P (1994) Learning practical knowledge Journal of F & HE 18 (1)

(Bloor & Butterworth, 1996: 49–51)

Critiques of 'reflection'

By the later part of the 90s, 'reflection' had become a standard feature of professional training and development. Critical theorists and sociologists have one set of explanations for the dominance of the concept: they see it as part of the 'commodification' of experience, where managers and assessors can demand that those they manage not only have to make public their subjective experience, but that they present it to be measured and assessed in a qualifications 'market'. Psychologists and learning theorists would use different explanations: they see it as being central to the developing research and literature on professional learning.

Those who have to apply such research in the field of initial training and professional development cannot ignore it, but have become unhappy with the proliferation in the use of the term, and the vagueness with which it is defined. It has become the 'hurrah' word for the decade – something that must always be a good thing, though no-one seems quite sure what it is. We need to take issue with this vagueness, and try to define its various applications more precisely, so that those in professional education can be more sure what they are demanding when they ask learners to 'reflect'.

The growth in the use of the concept of 'reflective practice' has coincided with a period during which Continuing Professional Development (CPD) has been highlighted as the key to keeping professionals up to date with continuing change, and an economic context in which on-the-job learning is increasingly the only kind available to employees.

Unfortunately, 'reflection' has become such a dominant term that it runs the danger of becoming just a fashionable slogan, attached to any CPD to give it currency. As the pendulum has swung inevitably back there is a growing number of writers who criticise Schön's work on various grounds: its lack of an empirically-tested base, the rare and highly specialised nature of the examples of teaching/coaching on which he based his theory, and lack of clarity and consistency in his own use of the key concepts: reflection-in-action and reflection-on-action. (For a brief analysis and summary of the critical perspective, see Eraut, 1994: 142–149). Such swings are simply the way in which knowledge proceeds, however. The familiar pattern of thesis (the theory is first put forward and becomes popular); antithesis (a backlash develops as the theory is subject to critical scrutiny, and its dominance is questioned); and synthesis (what remains of value if the theory becomes accepted on more secure grounds).

So it seems a good time to ask: what remains of lasting value in the idea of reflection? Those interested in the psychology of experiential learning, and in descriptions of professional effectiveness, still need terms to name the introspective operations that accompany skilful practical operations in complex situations. 'Reflection' seems as good a general term as any other – but it now needs to be treated as an 'umbrella' term; greater discriminations still need to be made.

Eraut's critique of Schön's work shows that even the man who launched the movement did not have a 'single coherent view' of reflection. The examples of teaching that Schön (1982) presented and analysed demonstrate not a single concept at work but rather a 'set of overlapping attributes'. Which of these attributes are relevant to the reflective writing and thinking that is now required in the training of many professionals?

They can be summarised, as the following list of guiding principles:

- the journal is an example of 'reflection-on-action' (rather than 'in-action'), so its proper focus is on the 'monitoring' aspects referred to above;

- because it is written after the experience (not during), it allows you more time to write more 'deliberatively', giving you a chance to explore options, consider alternatives, evaluate outcomes;

- in short, such writing is an analytical and critical process, looking at not just 'how did I go about my teaching/training?' but also asking 'how well did I do? are there different/more effective ways of achieving this? was it worth doing? for whom and why?'

These last questions are all examples of not just 'doing' the learning, but looking, as if from above, at the activity and analysing how the learning is done and assessing its value. These are the proper concerns of this kind of reflective writing.

References

Bloor M & Butterworth C (1996) 'The portfolio approach to professional development' in J Robson (ed) *The professional FE teacher* Avebury, pp44–59

Eraut M (1994) *Developing professional knowledge and competence* Falmer Press

Gibbs G (1988) *Learning by doing: a guide to teaching and learning methods* Further Education Unit

Kolb D (1984) *Experiential learning: experience as a source of learning and development* Prentice-Hall

Schön D (1982) 'The crisis of professional knowledge and the pursuit of an epistemology of practice' *Journal of Interprofessional Care* 6 (1)

8. The Reflective Practitioner: Mantra or Model for Emancipation?

Kathryn Ecclestone

Ecclestone begins by noting how widespread 'reflection' has become as an ingredient of programmes for PCET staff, and lists the possible types of reflective activity:

... We have no agreed paradigm for promoting 'reflective practice' in existing forms of professional learning. This is compounded by the lack of widespread debate about the underlying values and purposes of reflection in professional learning... This paper argues that current approaches to reflective practice are 'conceptually confused' and 'epistemologically ambiguous' (Hyland, 1994)...

Notions of the 'reflective practitioner' permeate the rationales and practice of over 70% of professional programmes in school teacher education (Furlong, 1995)... Munby and Russell ... examined how 'reflection' was interpreted in different teacher education programmes. Beyond a 'common-sense view' that reflection was beneficial, they found no '... shared sense of reflection to give shape to future developments...' (Munby & Russell, 1993)...

On many post-compulsory professional development programmes, 'reflection' can be almost anything connected loosely to professional learning in its broadest sense. In initial and in-service programmes for further and adult education (FAE) lecturers, reflection can encompass:

- a way of applying Kolb's learning cycle to reflect on and solve practical problems in the classroom
- a focus for evaluating professional practice against external criteria
- an in-depth and rigorous enquiry into professional practice, with a view to implementing change
- a rare and much-needed chance to compare practice and problems through structured and supportive discussion with peers
- an opportunity for disempowered complaining and negativity
- an exchange of practical teaching hints.

Course documents for different programmes reveal that the interchangeable use of the terms 'critical reflection' or merely 'reflection' can tacitly belie the different ideologies which can underpin reflective practice...

The author identifies two possible underlying ideologies, one from the competence movement, and one from the humanistic tradition:

Perhaps because 'reflection' and 'reflective practice' appear to cover any evaluative, thoughtful or systematic enquiry and almost any focus in professional practice, it has been so easily appropriated in NVQs for FAE teachers to become 'evaluation of practice' against externally defined criteria. The caveat that 'liberal' teacher educators might be able to imbue it with other, broader principles is often heard anecdotally at gatherings of post-compulsory educators.

But in a different vein, and from a different educational tradition, Knowles (1986: 82) argues that:

> *[Reflection] effectively challenges the thinking about events, circumstances and philosophies which constitute and value the status quo... [It] is seen as a means of emancipation and empowerment, a vehicle for allowing both teacher educators and teachers to take control of environment and circumstances in which they work and students learn...*

A belief in the importance of autonomy, independent thinking and challenge to existing forms of knowledge and practice has characterised andragogical approaches to adult education and higher education. Varying degrees of radicalism and liberalism might therefore underpin ideas about the educational purposes of reflection and the processes to foster and promote it. These values encourage learners to have the ability to participate in democratic decision-making, to see knowledge as being socially constructed and themselves as empowered agents of social change.

The focus of reflection therefore depends on underlying values: these are often tacit and it is questionable whether their implications for the types of reflective activity they foster are debated. A range of subjects and issues might therefore be used as the subject of different reflective processes:

- actions
- practical and theoretical reasons for action
- ethical justification for action.

Chown & Last (1993) argue that processes of reflection involve teachers in:

- recognising how they and others think about their experience
- acknowledging the values, beliefs, attitudes and specialist knowledge that they bring to situations
- identifying possible explanations and sources of new ideas and understanding
- formulating or trying out new courses of action
- changing what they do in light of this reflection...

It is clear then, 'reflective practice' is conceptually complex and has generated a vast amount of research and literature. It also has an uncertain place in the 'real life' of teachers at work in contrast to the more 'artificial' forms of reflection which they are often asked to engage in on initial and in-service courses (Eraut, 1995). This means that, in counteracting the NVQ alternative, reflective practice has become little more than what Ball (1994) refers to as 'mantric' theory. He suggests that much of the 'theory' we use to explore, explain and question issues and initiatives in educational research and debate has fallen victim to the 'wholesale appropriation of other "unreflective" and utilitarian languages' and 'intellectual isolationism' from other disciplines. He describes how theories can become 'mantras':

> *... theory can also work to provide comforting and apparently stable identities for beleagured academics in an increasingly slippery world... Too often ... theory becomes no more than a mantric reaffirmation of belief rather than a tool for exploration and for thinking otherwise. Such mantric uses of theories typically involve little more than a naming of spaces... The map simply needs to be coloured in rather than researched.*

It is questionable whether the implications of the different educational and social purposes of reflection, and their underlying values, are currently explored in detail in many post-compulsory professional learning programmes. Yet implicitly or explicitly, we convey certain purposes and benefits of reflective practice to learners on our programmes...

Forms and focuses of reflection might ... be different for novices in initial teacher training, and for more experienced teachers on in-service programmes. And reflection during formal learning is likely to be completely different from that which happens in ordinary professional life... Programme designers therefore need to consider the different outcomes that reflection should aim to achieve and which educational values and rationales these forms might implicitly reveal... Our models of practice and theory, whether articulated or not, usually reveal a tacit adherence to a set of values and assumptions about which the three traditions below are important...

- *Technical enquiry* draws on an empirical-analytic tradition based on the belief that teachers' subjective beliefs can be replaced with objective 'facts' and theory in order to assess current practice and find better practical alternatives... 'Reflective practice' would therefore encourage new lecturers to value the use of such theory in their practice. This 'theory' might be derived from books but Carr (1995) argues that it is increasingly being drawn from the observable and commonsense everyday practice of other teachers... It is most clearly manifested in NVQs where any reflection would focus on how well practitioners are achieving pre-defined outcomes.

- *Practical enquiry* [seeks] to improve the way in which teachers make professional decisions about their practice, and to help them articulate their concerns, implement new practices and think about the consequences of what they do. It provides a means for teachers to examine their everyday ideas and practices and to contribute to their repertoire of 'practical wisdom' (Carr, 1995). 'Reflective practice' stems from the idea that teachers are committed to understanding and developing their educational values in order to improve their practice... Activities focus on 'replay and rehearsal' (Louden, 1991) of classroom events or 'critical incidents', the use of narrative, biography and accounts of professional development to make sense of personal and professional experiences.

- *Critical enquiry* [as the basis for] 'reflective practice' encourages teachers to examine the contradictions between their own values and beliefs and the dominant social and institutional norms which govern their practice... Activities would involve systematic enquiry into how different stakeholders and social groups benefit from current practice, what personal and political action might secure change and how social structures inhibit or foster change...

Finally, Ecclestone recommends that education programmes for PCET staff should state the purposes of 'reflection' more clearly:

[This discussion] is based on the following premises:

1. The focus and purposes of reflection need to be made much more explicit than they currently are. They might need to be more structured and possibly more prescriptive for beginning and experienced teachers to experience different types of reflection with different purposes and values. If we do not do this, there is a danger that novice teachers in particular only experience fairly trivial or individualised concerns for reflection during their initial or in-service training or the over-prescriptive focus of NVQs. Novices might, however, initially need the rule-bound confines which a competence-based model offers...

2. As they become more expert, it is possible that teachers should be exposed to different rationales and models of development and to the different values which reflect progressive stages of development and expertise. This could include the more holistic and wide ranging focus of critical enquiry as well as the value-based focus of practical inquiry.

3. The range and scope of reflection and the outcomes they should encompass are an important matter for much wider debate in response to the rapid incursion of the authoritarian and bureaucratic outcomes in NVQs...

References

Ball SJ (1994) *Intellectuals or technicians: the urgent role of theory in educational studies* Annual address to the Standing Conference for Studies in Education, RSA London, 4th November

Carr W (1995) *For education: towards educational enquiry* Open University Press

Chown A & Last J (1993) 'Can the NCVQ model be used for teacher training?' *Journal of Further and Higher Education* 17, pp15–26

Eraut M (1995) 'Schön shock: a case for reframing reflection in action?' *Teachers and Teaching: Theory and Practice* 1, pp9–23

Furlong J (1995) *Mentoring student teachers* Routledge

Hyland T (1994) *Competence, education and NVQs: dissenting perspectives* Cassell

Knowles M (1986) *The adult learner – a neglected species* Gulf Publishing

Loudon W (1991) *Understanding teaching: continuity and change in teachers' knowledge* Cassell

Munby H & Russell T (1993) 'Reflective teacher education: technique or epistemology?' *Teaching and Teacher Education* 9, pp431–438

Part Three – The Policy Framework

The study of policy may be fascinating and frustrating, but living with the impact and consequences of policy decisions is less fascinating, less fun, and more frustrating (writes Ian McNay). Students and teachers, as scholars, have both of those experiences. The fascination, in study, for me, lies in three elements:

- the permeation of policy into everything: there are policy decisions at all levels from the personal to the international policy areas

- the unexpected (by policy makers at least) consequences of some policy decisions

- the constantly changing landscape: every new minister, or vice-chancellor, or principal, or head of a quango wants a policy initiative to be remembered by; events, anyway, constantly demand a policy response so there is little stability.

That is one of the frustrations, too. Whenever you feel you've got something pinned down, analysed and exemplified, something else changes. Even if you come close to understanding policy decisions and the principles behind them, the delivery of policy initiatives, the practices, the reality of experience, can be very different. There are several filters of interpretation and judgement, by professionals and others, between how policy is conceived by its creators and how it is then put into operation. Part of the frustration of practitioners is a feeling of lack of power to influence decisions at the stage of development of policy; part, for others, is a lack of power to control what is done. So, what is decided, and what is done, often differ.

Issues of autonomy and control, the concept of education professionals and their roles in a system of provision, are subject to decisions framed by sets of values held by key decision-makers. Sometimes these are overt. Government White Papers that described young trainees as 'tools of wealth creation' or saw the purpose of higher education as 'to serve the economy more effectively' were at one end of a spectrum of views from economic utilitarianism to liberal humanitarianism. Is the purpose of post-16 education to fit obedient people into slots, or to open their minds to a wealth of experience, knowledge and personal development? Arguments over the balance between these map on to debates about the relative merits of academic or vocational/professional provision. Each camp may make quality judgements on the other based on value positions – 'no earthly use, ivory towered, wishy washy' or 'no intellectual rigour, blinkered, unimaginative'. When people say, 'The truth is...' what follows is often opinion, not fact. You might use that as one test to judge what you read in the following pages. You might also look for times when statements reflect the values of the speaker or writer, though the values themselves are not articulated. They lie below the surface of a presentation. So, for example, government rhetoric is about lifelong learning – a liberal concept; yet all the targets for achievement in this policy domain are about work. Life, and learning – we may wish to believe – are about more than work.

I said earlier that policy permeated everything in post-compulsory education and training. Sir Toby Weaver split 'everything' into four domains:

1. access – who gets in?
2. curriculum – to study what and how?
3. resources – how funded?
4. structure – how organised and governed?

So *access* policy will be about expansion of provision, as the Blair government has promised; but it is also about widening the base of people who get in, as urged by the Kennedy Report on FE, the Dearing Report on HE, and the Fryer Report on Lifelong Learning. Yet access to education post-16 is still related to social class.

Curriculum policy embraces the academic/vocational debate (they are *not* mutually exclusive!). It also covers, for example, assessment policy and practices, the use of IT or study materials for flexible learning, modular schemes, key skills, and so on.

Resource policy is prominent in debates on value for money (another recurrent theme). Who covers the cost? How much post-compulsory education should the state provide free, given that the state benefits from a skilled workforce? How much should employers be expected to pay, or even forced to pay through a training levy? How much should individuals pay for courses, and are there some courses they should pay for more than others – postgraduate ones, for example, or 'leisure' adult education such as 'how to play bridge'? Levels of funding and how money is allocated are constantly disputed – within colleges, too, between central services and departmental provision, for example.

This brings us to *structures*. There is a complex set of organisations with diverse sources of money – from Europe, from different ministries or agencies, from local, regional and national funding bodies. There are organisations concerned with quality, others concerned with qualifications. New legislation is leading to new structures between the centre and the colleges, and new types of regional co-ordination in England, in Scotland and in Wales.

One key feature of the modern landscape is the use of legislation. There has been more of it in the past 20 or so years than in the previous 200. This 'corporate bureaucracy' implies value stances about how things should be, and many colleges reflect that environment. There is a conflict between the 'collegial' approach – emphasising individual professional freedom – and the 'managerialist' approach, with its emphasis on markets, product teams, and payment by results.

The readings in this Part (and indeed in Parts Four and Five) have been written or selected in order to help you explore such issues. Though the main focus is on recent and current policy related to vocational education and training, we hope that all readers will be able to use this to examine, explain, perhaps even understand, their own work context.

9. The Forgotten Sector

Bill Bailey

Introduction

Post-compulsory education and training (PCET) in England and Wales has often been referred to as the 'forgotten sector' of our educational provision. This is because it has never enjoyed the sustained attention of policy-makers, nor has it been the subject of high-profile educational debate, as has been the case with the schools sector or the universities. This neglect during much of the twentieth century has been reflected in the slow and patchy development of opportunities for post-compulsory education in this country (compared, for example, with countries like France and Germany) and the absence at any time of a coherent national plan or policy, backed by investment of public resources. Teachers and managers involved in further education have always felt they were working in a 'Cinderella' sector, which has never had the same status as schools providing for all the children in an area, or higher education colleges and universities offering degrees. Groups associated with further education colleges and other PCET institutions (like the teachers' unions and associations of principals for example) have often believed that their work and its value to students, and to society, have not been understood.

However, the neglect has not been total. Education legislation passed at the end of both world wars included provision for post-school education and training: the Acts of 1918 and 1944 provided for compulsory further education, on a part-time day release basis, respectively for 14–18 and 15–18 year olds. The purposes identified for this were the extension of general education and the development of vocational education for adolescents, but on each occasion post-war economic difficulties prevented the realisation of these schemes, with the interest of politicians reverting to developments in the schools. The political failure to see these plans through to implementation left its mark on the kind of opportunities available to young workers and adults. Instead of a national 'standard' provision of PCET – serving vocational and non-vocational needs in a unified and coordinated system – developments became piecemeal, reflecting particular and current pressures at local and national levels, and depending on the willingness of local education authorities (LEAs) and other agencies to maintain provision in their areas.

The historical inheritance of practitioners in the sector today is the variable and in some ways incoherent collection of institutions, bodies and agencies responsible for providing education and training after school, for designing vocational, professional and leisure courses and for awarding the qualifications that many of these lead to.

The world of PCET

One of the key characteristics of PCET has already been mentioned: its marginal status outside the mainstream of educational thinking and development. A second feature, in a way fundamental to the first, is its voluntary nature. It has always been voluntary (i.e. post-'compulsory') in the sense that all students have been volunteer attenders or, in some cases, have been sent on technical courses by the voluntary decision of their employers. This state of affairs has been reflected in the history of provision of further and adult education by local education authorities.

In the absence of any definition of an 'adequate' or minimum service of post-school further education and training the local authorities have varied in the level of their interest in, and in their expenditure on, the various types of PCET. As the LEA for the capital city the London County Council (and later the Inner London Education Authority) had a relatively highly developed provision from the early years of the century up to its abolition in 1989. The cities of Manchester, Birmingham and Glasgow, too, had large technical institutions a hundred years ago, while Sheffield had no separate technical or further education institution until well after the Second World War.

To argue that, as a consequence of its history, PCET provision is marginal, voluntary, and patchy or variable, is not to imply that in recent decades it has not expanded and developed or that many students have not taken advantage of opportunities. In fact, in further and adult education colleges and in voluntary and private agencies significant changes have taken place over the years. Whether these developments have been the result of deliberate national policy and whether they have led to changes in public or official perceptions and understanding of the world of PCET is a question for discussion. What is certain is that colleges offer a wide variety of provision.

The main kinds of work that colleges are currently involved in are these:
- vocational courses related to students' current or future employment
- general education, GCSE, GCE A level courses for 16–19-year-olds and adults (for 16–19-year-olds, colleges operate as alternative sixth forms)
- programmes, again for school-leavers or for adults, for students with learning difficulties and disabilities
- training programmes for unemployed school-leavers/adults, under the 16-hr rule, currently being replaced by the New Deal for 18–24-year-olds (and now to 50+)
- basic education provision: literacy and numeracy for adults and English as a Second Language for immigrants and refugees
- 'Access' courses to enable adults to enter higher education without traditional A level entry qualifications
- higher education courses taught wholly or in part at the colleges
- tailor-made and full-cost courses for local employers
- leisure and recreational courses, usually in association with the LEA.

This analysis of the work, or the 'offer' to local communities, of the colleges gives some idea of the diversity of the work of the main PCET institutions, the further education colleges. Although it is not exhaustive – it does not include training schemes in the branches of the armed forces or of the police, for example – it does give some impression of the wide range of work conducted by teachers in the institutions in the 'world of PCET'. It also reveals the complexity of PCET, which so often baffles those who have no personal experience of it. This can also be related to the issue of the low status of the sector, since it does seem that in order to have higher standing an educational institution in this country needs to have a clear focus and identity.

Recent changes in PCET

During the 1980s, when successive Conservative governments engaged in their educational 'reforms', there were many staff in PCET who believed that the changes did not concern them and their work. After all, their work was useful and relevant in meeting the needs of students and employers. Given governments' customary political priorities it was to be expected that they would focus on the schools – the compulsory years of education for all children. This is shown in the Education Reform Act (1988), which introduced the national curriculum 5–16, national testing, and the opportunity for schools in England and Wales to 'opt out' from LEA control.

In fact, at about this time an important development for vocational teachers was beginning to take shape, with the creation of the National Council for Vocational Qualifications (NCVQ), after the Manpower Services Commission (MSC) report in 1986. The unplanned growth of technical and further education had led to the existence of many examining and awarding bodies, whose certificates and diplomas worked to different standards, leading to confusion in the minds of employers and students who often failed to understand the nomenclature and the level of different qualifications.

The NCVQ's purpose was to set up a framework of qualifications into which all vocational qualifications would be placed. This five-level framework was established along with the adoption of the competence-based approach in an effort to ensure that qualifications indicated that their holders could efficiently perform the task at work. (Competences are supposed to be established by employers in the occupational area in which they are to be used.) For a review of the NCVQ's first ten years see Peter Robinson's *Rhetoric and Reality: Britain's New Vocational Qualifications* (Robinson, 1996). The influence of employers on vocational training had already been enhanced by the creation of the Training and Enterprise Councils; these employer-dominated bodies have, at the time of writing, the responsibility for stimulating training in order to promote their local economies.

The priority of government policies was clearly established in these initiatives: to make British industry more competitive in the new global market by improving the relevance and standards of vocational qualifications achieved by the workforce at all levels. This emphasis on serving the needs of the economy was continued in the White Paper (DES/DOE, 1991) which preceded the Further and Higher Education Act of 1992. It is worth noting that it was presented by Prime Minister John Major as part of the government's intention to recognise and build on the further education colleges' contribution to economic development – and so to enable these 'Cinderella' institutions at last to take their place in the mainstream educational system.

The Act set out to achieve this by 'incorporating' the colleges, that is by taking them out of LEA control and making their newly constituted governing bodies responsible for the conduct of their own affairs: the employment of staff, the management of buildings and other resources, and the supply of education and training through entering into contracts with other bodies. Thus, the link between the colleges and their local education authorities was broken.

For the first time, too, an attempt was made to define 'academic/vocational' as opposed to 'leisure-time' activities. Schedule 2 of the F&HE Act gave this list:

a) courses leading to vocational qualifications

b) GCSE or GCE A/AS levels

c) 'Access' courses preparing students for entry to courses of higher education

d) courses which prepare students for entry to courses listed in a) to c).

e) basic literacy in English

f) teaching English to students where English is not the language spoken at home

g) basic principles of mathematics

h) courses for proficiency or literacy in Welsh (Wales only)

i) independent living and communication skills for those with learning difficulties which prepare for entry to courses d) to g).

To replace the LEAs as the source of public funding for what became known as 'Schedule 2' work, Further Education Funding Councils (FEFCs) were set up, one for England and one for Wales. Adult and community education ('non-Schedule 2' work) remained, by and large, the responsibility of the LEAs, insofar as they wished to make such provision.

It is interesting to note that it was not very long before the two new 'funding' councils became very powerful quality assurance agencies for the inspection and assessment of colleges. Yet they, too, are set to disappear under the new legislation in the Learning and Skills Bill, 2000, together with the Training and Enterprise Councils.

References

Department for Education & Science/Department of Employment (1991) *White Paper: Education and training for the 21st century* (2 vols) HMSO

Manpower Services Commission (1986) *Review of vocational qualifications in England and Wales (the de Ville Report)* HMSO

Robinson P (1996) *Rhetoric and reality: Britain's new vocational qualifications* Centre for Economic Performance, London School of Economics

10.   1992 and All That: The F & HE Act 1992

Patrick Ainley & Bill Bailey

Going corporate

On 1st April 1993 the further education and sixth-form colleges were 'incorporated'. Under the Further and Higher Education Act of 1992 – the first major legislative recasting of FE since 1944 – they ceased to be part of local education authorities' responsibilities. Instead, newly constituted governing bodies, or 'corporations', became responsible for the assets, the staff and the management of their colleges. Appointed initially by 'search committees' led by Principals, these self-perpetuating college corporations have charitable status. They are, however, empowered not only to provide education and training but to supply goods and services, acquire and dispose of land and property, enter into commercial contracts and to borrow and invest, as long as this is 'incidental' to the provision of further education. The corporations may also include a student representative, although 106 of them do not. They also have the same right to commercial confidentiality as private companies, although college corporations are not covered by the Companies Act, and can appoint their own staff, setting the framework for pay and conditions without necessary reference to national norms. Their Principals have become Chief Executives working to the new governing bodies which, following the 1992 Act, have few if any, local authority representatives, including instead one nominee from the new employer-run Training and Enterprise Councils.

Colleges receive state money from Funding Councils – one for England, and another for Wales which also covers higher education. The 43 Scottish colleges are still funded from the Scottish Office, though there have been proposals to introduce a Funding Council for them too. [This has now been set in place.] Like the Funding Councils for HE, together with the Funding Agency for (opted-out) Schools, the FEFCs are representative of what the Chair of the Nolan Committee on standards in public life called 'the big quangos', which he numbered at 3,000 with 42,000 appointments to their boards (Radio 4, 16 May 1996). Instead of representatives from local authorities and the other stakeholders previously involved, the Secretary of State for Education appointed 13 large, private company representatives, like the first Chair of the FEFC who was a former Chief Executive of Boots the Chemist. As well as appointing its board members, the DfEE also has powers of 'guidance' and other reserve powers over the FEFC under the 1992 F&HE Act...

College corporations are amongst the 'little quangos' that Lord Nolan next went on to investigate. These include the (originally) 82 employer-led Training and Enterprise Councils (plus 22 Local Enterprise Companies in Scotland) which in 1991 were set up as private corporations to channel public funds to training agencies. In the case of college corporations, as independent individual agencies, they enter into contracts with the FEFC and other funding bodies to deliver services agreed in advance. Delivery is guaranteed by the achievement of various specified performance indicators. Responsibility for delivery is thus devolved downwards whilst power – if not overall control – effectively contracts to the centre. The new type of state, exemplified by the new governance of FE, is thus 'contracting' in two senses. As well as contracting with their funding councils, agencies like college corporations can in their turn contract out to other providers of services. Through these administrative and accounting arrangements the rigours of the market have been introduced – in FE as elsewhere – into previously local authority-run public services. The argument for this was that these services would be provided to their customers more cheaply, quickly, efficiently and responsively by a local – and national – state sector imbued not only with the ideology of enterprise but reorganised along the lines of the new, slimmed down, flexible, private sector in place of old and hierarchical bureaucracies.

The piecemeal process by which these new contracting arrangements were introduced is well illustrated by the government's decision to incorporate the colleges. This was clearly connected with the Treasury's need to quickly make up the £2 billion, which was lost through the Poll Tax revolt that helped to bring down Mrs Thatcher. This left her chosen successor, John Major, with the immediate task of finding another way to reduce local government expenditure. There was a precedent in the incorporation of the polytechnics and other colleges of higher education after the 1988 Education Act. Under their own Polytechnics and Colleges Funding Council (the PCFC), these higher education institutions increased the overall funding they received by raising their numbers of students by about a half (from 250,000 to 382,000 full-time students in the polytechnics alone), while their unit costs went down by about a quarter between 1989 and 1992. This impressive efficiency gain undoubtedly influenced the government as an example of what could be done with further education. In addition, an elaborate system of funding polytechnic courses at differential but nationally standard rates per student had been developed if not invented by the chief accountant to the PCFC, Roger McClure. He subsequently transferred to the FEFC along with his Chief Executive, Sir William Stubbs, previously of the Inner London Education Authority.

Moreover, further incorporations would also represent another inroad into the LEAs' stake or involvement in post-compulsory education, like the local management of schools and colleges also introduced by the 1988 Act. In this way incorporation can be seen as the continuation of a long-term strategy to remove state education and training, along with other public services, from local council control. It may also be seen as a further attack upon largely Labour-controlled local democracy, regarded by many of the [former] ruling Conservatives as inefficient if not corrupt. So, while it is true that incorporation of FE would probably have happened anyway, the Poll Tax debacle provided the opportunity to do then what would have been done later. Again, Kenneth Baker's memoirs recall that work had begun before he left the then-DES in 1989 to give the FE colleges the same 'independence' as the polytechnics.

The whole business, however, was rushed through, as a result of the immediate necessity to raise revenue. It was, as was said at the time, a notoriously 'quick fix'. In fact, with the additional uncertainties surrounding the result of the 1992 general election, some colleges and LEAs delayed preparation for incorporation, believing it would never happen because Labour would win the election. In its haste and its own uncertainty over re-election the government surprisingly included the sixth-form colleges in its plans for FE. Sixth-form colleges had always previously been seen as part of the school sector. This sudden inclusion was either a mistake by the then Education Minister Kenneth Clarke, or else it was a deliberate move to make up the balance still required to compensate for the Poll Tax shortfall. Whichever, the result was a chalk and cheese sector in which the future of many sixth-form colleges was for some time even more uncertain than the fate of the rest of the newly independent tertiary and FE colleges with which they now found themselves incorporated on terms of equality and competition.

Needless to say, government rhetoric brushed aside such anomalies. Kenneth Clarke – memorably described by David Triesman, then President of the college lecturers' Union NATFHE, as 'the only man who can swagger sitting down' – focused upon the key role colleges could now play in contributing to the National Education and Training Targets. These NETTs (later randomly mutated to NTETs) were first formalised for the UK by the major private employers' organisation, the Confederation of British Industry, at the prompting of the Organisation for Economic Co-operation and Development, a club of the richest industrialised countries. They set ambitious targets for both foundation learning in compulsory schooling and lifetime learning after it. These were expressed as percentages of the workforce (not the population as a whole), and were supposed to reach various levels by target dates.

Of course, these Targets had their own quango, a National Council which was responsible for setting and then revising them when they were not achieved. To meet these Targets, an increased number of young people over 16, and of adults, had to participate in education and training at all levels, so raising the proportion of qualified workers. To contribute to this process, White Papers preceding the 1992 Act made much of the need to recognise the colleges and to bring this Cinderella sector, as Clarke called it, into the mainstream of the education system by giving its colleges a new status, new management and by developing their curricula in line with the needs of a modernising economy.

Behind the government's wider justifications for the reform of further education was an awareness of the relatively poor performance of 16–19 education and training in the UK. There was also a recognition that the previous approach, based on the German model of separate schooling for a minority and Youth Training for a majority, which was tried from 1976 to 1987, had failed to address this problem. These criticisms were detailed in the joint report of the Audit Commission and the Office for Standards in Education, published in December 1993, which contrasted the low age participation rate in continuing education post-16 with other developed countries. For, while there had been a shift to what has been called a 'medium participation' post-compulsory education and training system, the rate of increase slowed and then declined for the first time for ten years from its peak of 72.6 per cent of all 16-year-olds in 1993 to 70.7 per cent by 1995. (Though the Heads of the Careers Services Association recorded the percentage staying on in 1995 at only 67.6 per cent.)

The recommendation of the Audit Commission/OFSTED Report was that steps be taken to ensure that public money was spent more effectively. There was at that time no attempt to collect reliable information on student enrolment and achievement on all FE courses, including 'drop-out' of students from them. The report alleged that typically between 30 and 40 per cent of all FE students failed to successfully complete the course on which they enrolled, so wasting £350 million a year. An even greater proportion failed to complete training courses run by TECs and LECs. In 1992, less than 30 per cent of YTS graduates had acquired a vocational qualification, and most of these were at the lower levels (i.e. at or below GCSE equivalent). Drop-out and failure on academic courses, particularly GCSE retakes but also A levels, were also high, even in sixth forms.

An early FEFC circular showed that costs varied considerably between colleges – for both academic and vocational students. These ranged from an average per student of £1,486 at Barnfield College in Luton to £5,579 at a typically expensive agricultural college, Kirkley Hall in Northumberland. These figures were, however, disputed by the colleges and others involved for ignoring other sources of funding and taking insufficient account of part-timers and other factors. There were also pronounced variations in class sizes and in the number of hours students were taught on the same courses in different colleges. These in turn bore little relation to student achievements in terms of the qualifications they obtained.

The English Further Education Funding Council, established by the 1992 Act, therefore took as its aims, as set out in its circular 93/12 of June 1993:

- to secure throughout England sufficient and adequate facilities for further education to meet the needs of students, including those with learning difficulties and disabilities, and the communities in which they live
- to contribute to the development of a world-class workforce as envisaged in the National Education and Training Targets
- to promote improvements in the quality of further education
- to promote access to further education by people who do not participate in education and training but who could benefit from it
- to ensure that the potential of the sector and its financial needs are properly represented at national level.

This was not a plan but a statement of indicative aims, though not as specific as the National Targets. As William Stubbs declared, the FEFC was not a planning organisation. So, while it can earmark for priority areas, the FEFC presides over a free market system. And, although it has powers to plan, the Council is not obliged to respond to the suggestions it receives from its nine regional committees as to the sufficiency of FE provision in their areas. As a FEFC spokeswoman was quoted as saying in the *Times Educational Supplement* (8 December 1995), 'It is a matter for colleges to decide what they offer and where. It is not for the Council to dictate what they should and should not be offering'. It is the colleges that attempt to plan.

The FEFC aimed to meet the criticisms of the previous approach to further education and training, and it was in the light of this critique that the new Council had been established to channel public funding to the colleges. The extent of the culture change which this new form of funding involved cannot be overestimated. The old world tended to be governed by a number of certainties that meant people felt they knew where they were. The new funding regime tore up this secure existence. The Principals became Chief Executives who were responsible for their budgets, the employment of their staff (teaching and support) and for the future of their 'business', the 'business' being the marketing of their courses and the recruitment and successful progress of their customers, the students. This was the new business of learning which the new funding method introduced.

It is in the area of funding that the 1992 Act has had its greatest impact, so that it is not an exaggeration to say that changes in the management, the organisation and the student experience of further education have been driven by the changes in funding...

Meanwhile, a second function of the FEFC is that of assessing the quality of further education by inspection. Again FE colleges, like schools, the former polytechnics and other local authority higher and adult colleges, had been subject to periodic inspection by Her Majesty's Inspectors of Education, an august professional body operating independently of the Department for Education under charter from the Crown. HMI were reconstituted by the Conservatives in 1992, by which time their whole-college inspections had in any case become rather rare. The FEFC therefore decided early in its existence to establish its own inspectorate comprising 70 full-time and 600 part-time inspectors, headed by a former Chief HMI, Terry Melia. As with inspections of schools by the new Office for Standards in Education (OFSTED), the aim was to inspect and report on all aspects of colleges' activities every four years. This is also proving too demanding and a system of self-assessment was therefore proposed. This would give colleges responsibility for monitoring their own standards. Inspections would then only occur for low-scoring colleges or curriculum areas within them. These arrangements have been postponed, although similar ones were suggested by the Higher Education Quality Council for its institutions.

By Spring 1996 approximately 200 colleges had been inspected. These visits resulted in reports on which the colleges based their 'action plans' for improvements and in summary reports which covered aspects of management, as well as all curriculum areas in all colleges. All aspects of a college's activity are graded by the inspectors from 1 ('many strengths and few weaknesses') to 5 ('many weaknesses and few strengths'). The grades are then taken into account by the Funding Council when deciding on a college's future funding. For example, a curriculum area which received a 4 or 5 grade in the inspection will not be allocated additional students, or rather 'units', until it has been reinspected and provided evidence that weaknesses have been corrected.

11. Current Policy Initiatives

Ken Marsh & Amanda Snowden

In June 1999 New Labour published the White Paper *'Learning to Succeed – a new framework for post-16 learning'*. In that document (DfEE, 1999a: 21) the government set out its reasons for seeking a rationalisation of the post-compulsory sector. It asserted that the former marketised approach had led to too much duplication, confusion and bureaucracy, with an absence of effective co-ordination or strategic planning. The whole system as it stood lacked innovation and flexibility and fell short of the principles needed to deliver lifelong learning as set out in *'The Learning Age'* (DfEE, 1998).

The White Paper (now incorporated into the Learning and Skills Bill, 2000) sets out an extended vision of the 'learning age' in seeking innovative and rationally planned ways to deliver lifelong learning to meet the challenges of technological and economic change in an increasingly competitive and globalised world. The White Paper and the subsequent Bill also embodied some of the recommendations on widening participation set out in the Kennedy Report *'Learning Works'* (FEFC, 1997) and links into the post-16 qualifications reform proposals 'Curriculum 2000' proposed in the consultation paper *'Qualifying for Success'* (DfEE, 1997).

The Bill proposes bringing into being in April 2001 a new body called the Learning and Skills Council for England, which will replace both the Further Education Funding Council (FEFC) and the Training and Enterprise Councils (TECs). This body will operate through a devolved network of 47 local Learning and Skills Councils and will be responsible for the funding, planning and quality assurance of all post-16 and adult education and training, including work-based learning, in England. In Wales, similarly, the FEFCW and the Welsh TECs will be replaced by a new National Council for Education and Training for Wales.

The Learning and Skills Council remit will include:

- striving to improve the quality and relevance of post-16 learning

- forging strong links between learning and commerce

- creating partnerships with local authorities, the voluntary sector, trade unions and the Youth, Careers and Employment services, and Investors in People

- providing a comprehensive network of advice, guidance and support for both 16 to 19 and adult age groups (using the University for Industry/Learning Direct)

- developing a new integrated youth support service, the Connexions service, and a network of Learning Mentors, to advise and guide young people, 13 to 19

- supporting unemployed people and those with special learning needs back to work through learning

- rationalising existing inspection arrangements (16–19 inspection by OFSTED, post-19 by a new Adult Learning Inspectorate to replace the existing Training and Standards Council)

- setting up a 16–19 Young People's Learning Committee and an Adult Learning Committee to provide information and feedback to the Learning and Skills Council and so lead to an improvement in quality of provision and help achieve the Government's National Education and Training Targets

- taking over from the TECs full responsibility for work-based training

- providing strategic planning and funding for the whole post-16 vocational education and training sector (excluding higher education)

- liaising with the Regional Development Agencies, whose representatives will sit on the boards of the LSCs and have powers to approve plans or otherwise.

It might, in passing, be worth asking how far the learners' interests will be represented in this scheme, to substantiate the White Paper's 'learner-led' rhetoric.

A changing world

The background to the drive to reform the post-16 sector has been one of great social and technological change where workplace skills, it is claimed, are changing at a rapid pace. The fear of falling behind our EU competitors is pushing the current government to a more statist/interventionist approach in the delivery of education and training. The continued reluctance of employers in the UK to go beyond rhetoric and take on some responsibility for training the nation's workforce, together with a perceived national reluctance on the part of individuals to engage in education and training after leaving school, have forced the government's hand in its attempt to set up a coherent national framework for a locally planned and delivered system of post-16 education and training. The current buzzword is 'partnership' between all those concerned with training the nation's workforce in the government's drive to create a learning society. Reading between the lines of these reforms we might observe a tacit admission that despite 20 years of intervention by national governments in post-16 and adult education and training, the system is still incoherent and failing to deliver.

Business

The individual LSCs are to liaise with local interested parties by creating learning partnerships between the world of business, the local authorities, the voluntary sector, the Employment Service etc. in order to plan to meet the learning and training needs of local labour markets and communities. The LSCs will encourage business links with the post-16 education and training sector so that employers will have some influence on the types of learning on offer and, together with trade unions and local authority representatives (now back in favour), will be represented on the boards of the LSCs. Again one might question any claims of a return to real democratic processes in that the boards – from which learners are once more excluded – will be appointed not elected.

Lifelong learning through the individualisation of learning

The Bill heralds what the Secretary of State called a 'step change in our learning and skills performance'. It claims to seek to individualise learning programmes so that it is the 'learner' who drives the education/training machine and not the provider. Education and training programmes are to be delivered flexibly to suit learners' needs and time constraints. People should be able to learn at home or in the workplace or in learning centres convenient to them. The University for Industry (UfI) is to have a significant role to play here. Government policy as expressed in the Bill also includes the promotion of 'Individual Learning Accounts' to aid funding for those seeking to upskill or continue their education and training, with tax breaks for employers who contribute funding to employees' individual learning accounts. Personal advisers on New Deal will seek to ensure that the unemployed are rescued from a dependency culture and linked into education and training opportunities.

Adult learners: a comprehensive approach

The Moser Committee reported in *'A Fresh Start'* (DfEE, 1999b) that seven million adults have no formal qualifications and over one in five of all adults in the UK have real problems with literacy and numeracy. The Learning and Skills Bill claims to inject new drive and vigour into its lifelong learning and inclusion support programmes. In addition to individual learning accounts, the national Learning and Skills Council, together with those organisations it funds, will work with broadcasters, the media, the UfI, the National Institute of Adult Continuing Education (NIACE) and others in the private and voluntary sector to promote the value of learning to people and the benefit it can bring to their lives.

The 1999 White Paper announced that the responsibility for work-based learning for adults will move to the Employment Service from April 2001 in order to achieve a greater integration of the skills agenda with the Welfare to Work and New Deal Programmes. The Employment Service is currently working with the DfEE on a review of New Deal 25+ provision. The outcome of the review will influence the shape of work-based learning for adults after April 2001.

Planning and advice

Spreading the word about learning and training opportunities is viewed as essential. The Learning and Skills Bill envisages that all adults will have access to information, advice and guidance through a national network offering free information and staffed by trained personal advisers. The national helpline 'Learning Direct' is already in place: launched in February 1998 it expects to handle 1.5 million calls annually by 2002. For the 13–19 age group the new youth service, 'Connexions', will provide support and impartial careers information, and seek to raise individual expectations. It will seek to treat the student as a whole person, looking at individual needs and providing mentoring support where necessary for those considered at risk of social exclusion in the transition from school/college to work.

A new inspectorate

The Learning and Skills Bill sets up a new inspection framework and a new and controversial division in education and training. OFSTED will have responsibility for the inspection of all education provision up to 19 and an Adult Learning Inspectorate will be established to cover post-19 education and training, including work-based learning. This new post-19 division is interesting in that it seems that 16–19 education and training is more and more likely to take place in larger sixth form colleges, as smaller schools' sixth forms are seen to be uneconomic and limited in their curriculum offer.

FE colleges, as they take in more adult learners and trainees who have 'failed' the academic National Curriculum, may come to resemble American Community Colleges offering flexible progression routes into HE. The establishment of two-year foundation degrees provided in the colleges is now under serious discussion, as a means to achieving the government's targets for increasing participation in higher education

A reformed qualifications framework – Curriculum 2000

The White Paper draws on the recommendations of the consultation paper *'Qualifying for Success'* (DfEE 1997) which in turn sought to rationalise, simplify, broaden and build progression routes across the existing jungle of post-16 qualifications.

Key curriculum changes in England and Wales which are intended to be in place by 2001 are:

- a new AS level to encourage take-up of more subjects in addition to the usual A levels;

- world-class tests within the A level system to stretch the most able;

- linear and modular A level courses in all subjects with strict limits on coursework and an insistence on synoptic tests at the end of all courses;

- upgraded and more flexible GNVQs to enable more students to pursue a mix of academic and vocational subjects post-16 (Scotland has being doing this for a number of years);

- a new key skills qualification to encourage all young people to continue to enhance their skills after the age of 16 in communication, IT, and the application of number;

- for adults, there will be the opportunity to take mixed units of study based on standards set up by the National Training Organisations; the misguided Schedule 2 funding division between vocational and recreational courses set up in the 1992 Further and Higher Education Act is to be ended, though 'priority of funding support will still be given to those adults working towards a nationally recognised qualification' (which sounds a lot like keeping the vocational/recreational division).

Some final reflections

The search for more coherence and accountability in post-16 provision is laudable, as is the support envisaged to establish a learning culture and a more rational qualifications framework. The idea that it is the learner who should drive the system is also something of a revolution, though with little amount of learner representation on the key bodies one might be forgiven for thinking this is rhetoric only. One might also feel a little uneasy at what appear to be solely economic ends to which these reforms are directed.

As noted earlier the White Paper states that priority of funding will go to those adults working towards a nationally recognised qualification. What of the old adult education values of the intrinsic worth of education and its recreational aspects, i.e. the liberal or liberating and creative dimensions of adult education? Is it really the Government's intention to end this division between the recreational and vocational or is it a softening only? The pressures on the colleges also to deliver this reformed flexibility are immense, particularly so in their marketised state. In their drive to cut costs many colleges are now managing on a largely casualised, part-time staff with core staff suffering from innovation fatigue. The sector needs more funding and stability for it to deliver. Has 'joined-up-thinking' omitted thinking about the deliverers of New Labour's lifelong learning vision and is lifelong learning to be only conceived as 'work-long learning'?

References:

DfEE (1997) *Qualifying for success: a consultation paper on the future of post-16 qualifications* The Stationery Office

DfEE (1998) *The learning age – a renaissance for a new Britain. Cmnd 3790* The Stationery Office

DfEE (1999a) *White Paper: Learning to succeed – a new framework for post-16 learning* The Stationery Office

DfEE (1999b) *Improving literacy and numeracy: a fresh start: Report of the working group chaired by Sir Claus Moser* The Stationery Office

FEFC (1997) *Learning works: Report of the Widening Participation Committee, chaired by Helena Kennedy QC* Further Education Funding Council

Part Four – Qualifications and the World of Work

The major part of the post-16 sector has traditionally been focused on the preparation of workers for the labour market. The contributions in Part Four will provide a comprehensive and critical account of the sometimes arbitrary development of schemes to provide vocational education and training to young people and adults over the last twenty or so years.

It often seems to be little more than a jungle of initials – UVP, YOPS, YTS, YT, CPVE, TVEI, not to mention CSE, GCE, GCSE, KS4, NVQs and GNVQs. Geoff Stanton clears a way through some of this undergrowth and leads us towards an understanding of the processes of decision making. It is only possible to make an informed judgement on more recent schemes like the New Deal if we have some comprehension of the fumbling way in which policy initiatives in the past have been devised, together with a recognition that many of the issues are never resolved but keep coming back in a different form.

Prue Huddleston and Lorna Unwin look at it, in part, from the point of view of the structure of society and the supposed division of the labour market into three categories of employees: professional, skilled and unskilled. This not only mirrors the attempt of the 1944 Education Act to set up three types of secondary school – grammar, technical and modern – but goes back to Plato's division of society in the 5th century BC into 'guardians', 'soldiers' and the 'common people'. Huddlestone and Unwin explore the roles of the significant stakeholders in vocational education and training, and explode the myth of employer involvement in policy making. They consider whether the perceived value of the qualifications currently on offer may also represent a tripartite division into 'academic, applied and vocational'.

Karen Evans and her colleagues bring the record up to date by questioning how far the actions of the Labour government since 1997 has made a significant contribution to the work-related learning of young people and adults. They are particularly critical of the pressures exerted on school leavers to enter low-quality jobs with few prospects of improvement in order to meet government employment targets.

Ken Marsh concludes this Part with the report of a piece of small-scale research into college perceptions of the New Deal, indicating a wide variety of ways in which the scheme can be operated.

12.   Patterns in Development

Geoff Stanton

Imagine a situation in which a car company decides that its model range requires completely revamping. Its vehicles still sell, and are being continually if gradually improved, but international competition is showing them up. The company therefore commissions three new models, each of which is intended to mark a departure from the past. They come on stream at different times but each embodies innovative design features, and aims to provide a step change in performance.

Unfortunately, events do not develop as intended. Complaints pour in, not only from customers, but also from the garages which sell and maintain the vehicles. Each vehicle has been designed and produced by a different division of the company, and each division struggles to put things right. The Divisional Heads are replaced, and in some cases the divisions themselves are re-organised. It is argued (whether by the divisions or by the parent company it is not altogether clear) that the new models are basically fine, and that the problems derive from users being reluctant to change or failing to understand the innovative features. However, attempts to improve the marketing of each model does not stem the complaints.

The task of the marketing people is not helped by the fact that the company directors and their families themselves continue to use a vintage model which is preserved from change, and does not adopt the innovative approaches which are causing some of the problems.

Finally, the parent company calls in third parties to undertake fundamental reviews of each of the new products. This leads to their recall and redesign.

While this process is still underway, it is realised that there is also a more general problem, resulting from the facts that each model has been designed independently, and that the vintage model continues in production. Customers cannot understand how they relate, or how their characteristics and purposes differ, and the garages find that even parts that perform identical functions have different designs and even names.

Eventually, the most high profile of the third parties, the Dearing Corporation, is given the task of reviewing the whole range.

Had this all indeed happened in a commercial context, the company would not have been satisfied simply to remedy the problems, it would have wanted to know what was going wrong and why it kept happening. Was it to do with the mismanagement of change? Did all three new models share similar design faults?

This chapter attempts to undertake this analysis with regard to the design and implementation of three initiatives:

- the National Curriculum (NC) , and especially key stage four (KS4)
- National Vocational Qualifications (NVQs)
- General National Vocational Qualifications (GNVQs).

In other words, I shall be asking 'Why is it that three of the most significant developments in post-14 education and training in the last decade proved to be unmanageable when first introduced?' To have this happen once might be thought to be a misfortune. Three times looks like a systems fault from and about which we are failing to learn.

There were, of course, other initiatives which made considerable impact on 14–19 provision during the eighties.

These included the Certificate of Pre-vocational Education (CPVE), introduced in 1983 to rationalise and improve courses for the increasing number of young people who wished to stay on in education beyond the end of the compulsory schooling at 16, and the Youth Opportunities Programme (1978), and its successor from 1983 onwards, the Youth Training Scheme (YTS).

In the current employment market it is salutary to recall that there was also a scheme which started in 1978 for those many 16-year-olds who were employed but who received no systematic education or training. These schemes of Unified Vocational Preparation (UVP) were thought by many of those involved to embody a range of exciting and effective approaches to the needs of a difficult target group. Interestingly, in view of the more recent preoccupation with qualifications and testing, UVP focused on new approaches to the learning *process*, and to the role of teachers, youth-workers, workplace supervisors – and the learners themselves – within it.

The most comprehensive and well resourced initiative was TVEI – the Technical and Vocational Education Initiative – which was intended to affect all 14–19-year-olds in time and which continued in reduced form until 1997.

It is worth taking a slightly closer look at TVEI, because of the way it set about promoting change. Despite the fact that it was aimed at full-time students, TVEI was administered by the ministry concerned with employment and training, rather than the ministry concerned with education. This may have been partly because the officials and ministers concerned were thought to have the right kind of initiative in more senses than one, but it was also for a very good constitutional reason. The Education Ministers administered a system in which crucial decision-making was devolved to Local Education Authorities. They could indicate that an element of the local authority grant was intended for a given purpose, but they could not ensure that LEAs spent it that way, or even that it all reached the education budget. The local council might have other pressing priorities.

Any other ministry, by contrast, could enter into contracts with LEAs, and just as they could with any provider of services to them they had the legal power to see that the money was spent as the contract specified. In the light of later developments, it is interesting to recall how this was handled.

There was no centrally devised master plan at an operational level. Instead, those responsible for TVEI specified the aims they wished to see achieved, and invited schools, colleges and LEAs to propose ways of achieving them. This empowered energetic and imaginative practitioners. Indeed, some comparatively junior staff achieved local significance very quickly because of their ability firstly to construct plans which the funding body recognised as having potential, and secondly to deliver them effectively.

Therefore, although there were common national objectives, differing schemes were designed to achieve them locally. In order to be approved for funding, a scheme was required to show how staff and organisational development was being introduced to support curriculum changes, how changes were to be evaluated, and to explain how any innovation fitted into and would permanently enhance the local pattern of provision.

The philosophy and power of the TVEI approach was perhaps best encapsulated in the annual planning and review meetings, at which representatives of a local scheme would meet with central officials to review the working of the contract and consider the terms of its renewal. Local managers would be held to account for the achievement or otherwise of the objectives they themselves had proposed a year earlier, but they would also have a chance to raise technical and policy issues for the central officials to tackle.

In my view, this was a powerful and effective mechanism for change, and for balancing national priorities with the use of local innovation and special facilities. TVEI also recognised the importance of evaluation, and of balancing curriculum development, staff development and organisational development.

However, there were also problems. In particular, change appeared to be rather slow and somewhat messy, and there were difficulties in matching new learning programmes with existing qualification systems. Perhaps as a result, the pendulum swung, and we entered an era in which educational reform became equated with qualifications reform, and initiatives took the form of detailed schemes drawn up by central government or its agencies.

This was made possible by the Education Reform Act of 1988, which gave the Department of Education and Science the right to specify what was provided in the state sector of education for children of 5 to 16, whether with its money or that of the LEA.

Unfortunately, these new powers were then deployed without sufficient attention being paid to what was already known (not least from schemes such as TVEI) about:

- mechanisms for the effective management of educational developments
- the need to be clear about the relationship between qualifications and the curriculum

- the importance of any initiative as part of a larger system.

Finally, mention should be made of the introduction of the General Certificate of Secondary Education (GCSE), which took place from 1992 onwards, although it had been under discussion for many years previously. Possibly because of these extended discussions between practitioners and policy makers, and the parallel development of staff and materials, it has proved a remarkably effective innovation. However, the inability of policy makers to consider education as a system produced problems about the interface between GCSE and post-16 qualifications and – as we shall see – between GCSE and the overall National Curriculum.

The National Curriculum

The Government's Consultation Document on the National Curriculum 5–16 was issued in July 1987, and required responses by the end of September. The National Curriculum was implemented by the Education Reform Act 1988, and the National Curriculum Council (NCC) was established in August 1988, along with the Schools Examinations and Assessment Authority (SEAC). Even before that, two subject working groups, on mathematics and science, had been meeting. Their final reports coincided with the formation of the Council.

Therefore, before the Council even existed it had been decided that the curriculum was to be developed, and phased in, subject by subject. This meant that some of the later subject working groups could benefit from the difficulties of the earlier ones, but it is likely that this subject by subject approach derived less from a considered decision than from the fact that many of the politicians, officials and subject specialists involved could conceive of no other way of proceeding. For them, it was obvious that attainment targets, teaching schemes, and testing all had to be subject-based. That was their personal experience, and how else could it be?

The schedule provided for the first of the ten national curriculum subjects to be introduced for five-year-olds (Key Stage One) in 1989, and the last ones for the same age group in 1992. For 14-year-olds (Key Stage Four) all ten subjects would be phased in between 1992 and 1995.

The first Chairman and Chief Executive of the NCC, Duncan Graham, had previously chaired the maths working group, and has noted:

> *We were conscious that the science group was also meeting but we were all far too busy to meet each other. This was most unfortunate. A sharing of knowledge and some jointly formulated definitions of attainment targets would have reduced the incompatibilities which surfaced later.*
>
> (Graham & Tytler, 1993)

Many responses to the original consultation document had advised strongly that the curriculum should be planned as a whole rather than being designed a subject at a time. A few years earlier HMI had published a report on the whole curriculum which analysed it in terms of areas of knowledge, but government appeared to be in no mood to pay great heed to those who were responsible for the current system, and tended – perhaps understandably in the light of some of their previous experiences – to interpret arguments about things being more difficult than they seemed as delaying tactics.

The subject-based approach may have worked for secondary schools, where cynics said that only the pupils had to engage in and understand the curriculum as a whole, but primary school staff found themselves at the receiving end of what seemed like a never ending series of subject-based national curriculum orders, each of which took its own line and few of which acknowledged the potential and problems deriving from the fact that the staff and students were dealing with other subjects in parallel. As Sir Ron Dearing pointed out, referring to the assessment requirements for 7-year-olds:

> *A classroom teacher at Key Stage 1 with 35 pupils ... would (need to) make and record some 8,000 judgements. Statistics like these illustrate why many teachers feel that the current approach causes administrative overload...*
>
> (Dearing, 1993a)

If the problem for primary schools came in part from a failure to see the national curriculum itself as a system, the problem at Key Stage Four (the curriculum for 14–16-year-olds) came from a failure to relate the national curriculum to other systems.

Duncan Graham has stated that his deputy Peter Watkins (who had been a Secondary School Head) persuaded him of the incompatibility of the ten subject National Curriculum and the GCSE examinations as early as June 1988. He also claims that their initial attempts to raise the problem with civil servants met with *'the most discourteous reception, the first indication that no matter how justified proposals were they would not get very far if they were out of tune with current official thinking.'* According to Graham's admittedly partial view, this thinking had at least two aspects: that they were *'rocking the boat'* by questioning the *'fundamentals of something which was perfect in origin'*; and that there was plenty of time before Key Stage Four was to be introduced (whereas Graham and Watkins were all too aware of the lead time required for educational change).

After a number of interim solutions were put forward by NCC and Ministers (who differed), the issue was addressed in Sir Ron Dearing's wide-ranging review of the National Curriculum and its assessment in 1993.

Dearing's final report commented that *'despite action already taken by the Government, more flexibility was needed in Key Stage 4'* (Dearing, 1993b: para 5.1). Dearing identified policy issues as well as an implementation problem. Two of them were:

- whether Key Stage 4 was to be seen not as an *'educational terminus'* but rather as *'the beginning of a distinct phase which runs through to 19'* (para 5.7)

- whether the ten level scale was compatible with the GCSE grading system (paras 7.61 – 7.64).

The fact that these questions were being asked in 1993, six years after the first consultation document on the National Curriculum, and one year after Key Stage 4 was implemented, is powerful evidence of the original failure to see KS4 as part of a wider system. Even in 1993, the problem was only seen in terms of the problems which had arisen within KS4 itself. Although there was discussion of how to incorporate elements of the newly introduced GNVQs, there was no real mention of how KS4 related to A-levels and NVQs. It was not until the next Dearing Report, in 1996, that there was talk of a framework within which to place all national qualifications (Dearing, 1996b).

National Vocational Qualifications (NVQs)

The development of NVQs roughly paralleled that of the National Curriculum in terms of dates, but not in terms of all of its approach or assumptions.

The National Council for Vocational Qualifications was set up in 1986, two years earlier than the NCC, as a result of a Review of Vocational Qualifications chaired by Oscar DeVille. In his introduction to the report, he said: *'I believe that the 14–19 age group should increasingly be seen as a whole ... and that the "divide" between vocational and academic learning should be bridged'* (DeVille, 1986). However, his brief was confined to vocational qualifications, for which he proposed a National Framework with five levels. The levels spanned from operative through craft and technician functions to junior and senior management. As with the national curriculum two years later, each level was to be given a number. So at the very time that the national curriculum was designating (for instance) level three as representing the achievement of an average seven-year-old, NCVQ was already using the same number to represent vocational performance approximately equivalent to that reached by 18-year-olds gaining a couple of A levels.

There were other similarities which were nevertheless presented in crucially different ways. As with the National Curriculum two years later, NVQs were to offer greater clarity about the intended outcomes of learning. However, whereas for NVQs these outcomes were called *standards of competence* in the NC they were *statements of attainment*.

There were also important differences. NVQ competences were grouped into *units*, reflecting occupational functions, whereas the national curriculum was strongly subject-based. Whereas the National Curriculum placed for the first time a legal obligation on all state schools to implement a certain curriculum, the introduction of NVQs followed a period during which government had disbanded most Training Boards, which had imposed a compulsory levy on firms above a certain size in order to fund training. NVQs were to be adopted voluntarily, and in order to encourage this 'lead bodies' representing sectors of employment were to be given the right to specify what they wanted to see as the required standards. The 1986 White Paper specified that the first qualifications designated as NVQs should be available by summer 1987, and that the framework for the first four levels should be operational by 1991 (HMSO, 1986).

Although everyone now refers to NVQs as (radically) new qualifications, both the DeVille Report, and the subsequent White Paper, apply the label 'NVQ' to the national *framework*. Qualifications were intended to become NVQs, rather than an NVQ becoming a new qualification. As the White Paper said '... *this framework should be designed to incorporate and embrace existing qualifications ...'* This would have meant setting the criteria for inclusion in the framework rather loosely at first, tightening them up in order to bring greater coherence as quickly as experience, and perhaps the market, allowed. In fact, the reverse happened, with initially very strict conditions having to be relaxed as problems of implementation were encountered.

Although, in the early years, some existing qualifications were provisionally accredited as NVQs, for the most part the requirements were so detailed and so strictly applied that brand new qualifications had to be designed. This produced a situation in which innovative but untried qualifications found themselves in competition with others which might have required updating but already had recognition and currency. Partly because of this, and the need to develop standards for each occupation, the new qualifications came on stream more slowly than anticipated, and some of the initial awareness-raising amongst employers and colleges fell rather flat when the relevant qualifications turned out to be not yet available.

However, by 1990 there were about 130 Lead Bodies, with a further 20 in the process of being set up. They varied immensely in size and scope (from engineering to envelope manufacture, and from hairdressing to museums), and they had considerable freedom with regard to *what* they defined as standards of competence for their sectors. There was, however, considerable rigidity about *how* standards were to be defined, and the related qualifications were required to test every element of the standards, no more and no less.

This rigidity with regard to technical matters extended to other things. For instance, it was decided by NCVQ officials that:

- requirements for knowledge and understanding did not need to be separately specified, since they were implied by the ability to perform competently;
- the written specifications could be made so precise that competent performance would be reliably interpreted by all assessors, as long as they had the relevant NVQ assessors' qualification;
- in order to ensure that no candidate would be barred from gaining a qualification because of an inability to access a formal course, no syllabus or learning processes would be specified;
- since an employee was either competent or not, the qualification should be pass/fail, with no grading.

This has resulted in standards written in a way which employers and employees find difficult to understand, qualifications which can fail to correspond to the differing 'shapes' of similar jobs with different employers, and certification which does not always facilitate progression. Possibly as a result, take-up continues to give rise to concern.

It was intended that by 1995 NVQs would have largely replaced traditional vocational qualifications, as well as having filled the gaps where no qualifications were available (see NCVQ, 1990). In fact, in 1995 City and Guilds, the awarding body which had certificated the majority of NVQs, was expressing disappointment in the *'continuing slow growth of NVQs, in which we have invested heavily'* (CGLI, 1995). At the same time, the market for C&G's traditional qualifications remained buoyant. Similarly, in 1991 the then Junior Minister was saying *'In a very short space of time, NVQs will dominate the vocational provision offered by FE Colleges'* (Eggar, 1991a). However, in 1995 the FE Funding Council was reporting that of the qualifications it funded in English colleges only 8% were NVQs, compared (for instance) to 18% A levels and even 9% GCSEs. GNVQs were only 4% at that time. It was estimated that the majority of the remaining 60% of qualifications funded were other vocational qualifications (see Association for Colleges, 1996). The market which NVQs were designed to satisfy seemed to be signalling that something was wrong.

This was the background against which the Review of 100 of the most used NVQs and SVQs was commissioned from Gordon Beaumont in 1995/6 (Beaumont, 1996). It was noticeable, however, that the report did not fully admit or quantify the problem. Indeed, the evidence from NCVQ reported *'significant rates of expansion across all occupational areas and at all levels'* (NCVQ/SCOTVEC, 1996). It was not pointed out that the rate of growth was slowing down. Mention of take up varying between sectors concealed the fact that 43 NVQs (out of 734) accounted for over 80% of all awards (a significant number remaining unused), and that the majority of NVQs were awarded in service occupations, such as hairdressing (where one NVQ accounted for almost 8% of all NVQs ever awarded) and retail distribution, where previously many employees had been unqualified (see Robinson, 1996). Though important in themselves, such occupations make little contribution to the oft mentioned matter of the UK's international competitiveness.

On the other hand, employers and others clearly like the outcomes-based approach, and the grouping of them into units. Beaumont's suggestion that NVQs should increasingly be composed of core units plus a choice of optional units will certainly make the product more flexible and attractive. He is also right to require that standards should be written in plain language, but seems to assume that present problems derive simply from unnecessary use of jargon, rather than from the attempt to make the specifications completely unambiguous.

General National Vocational Qualifications

In the late eighties it was being assumed that the National Curriculum would provide a uniform diet for all of compulsory school age, and that all post-16 qualifications that were not GCSEs or A levels would become NVQs. By the early nineties, it was being realised that not all vocational provision could meet the NVQ criteria, particularly if the learners were not yet employed. Such learners needed a broad vocational preparation, whereas NVQs were occupationally specific, and many NVQs required access to the workplace for the valid assessment of the specified standards.

The need to develop a coherent range of *general* vocational qualifications was flagged up in the 1991 White Paper (HMSO, 1991). In May 1991 Ministers wrote to NCVQ to ask them to co-ordinate the necessary work. NCVQ issued a consultation paper in October, in the following September the first five vocational areas were piloted, at two levels, and they were fully implemented from September 1993.

It does not take much thought to see how strenuous (some might say ludicrous) this schedule was. Colleges, for instance, start recruiting students for the following September early in the calendar year. In order to offer applicants proper guidance, the general shape of any new provision has to be known by then, and for quality provision the teaching plans and learning materials have to be drawn up, and the course timetabled and staffed, between Easter and the summer break. In the case of GNVQs, the pilot schemes could not even be designed by NCVQ until the close of the consultation period in December, and the schemes proper had to be planned before the pilot period which followed was half completed.

There might have been some chance of this working if NCVQ had stuck to the original brief, which was to *'design the framework and the criteria for GNVQs ... and to invite ... awarding bodies to develop GNVQs which meet these criteria.'* Although it was requested by ministers that the first GNVQs should be accredited in time to be available in colleges and schools from September 1992 it was suggested by them that *'it should be possible to make rapid progress towards modifying some existing qualifications to bring them in line with the new criteria very quickly, and accrediting them'* (Eggar, 1991b).

What happened was that, once again, NCVQ set about designing a radically new qualification from scratch, adapting the approach which was already giving rise to unacknowledged problems with NVQs. Problems were exacerbated by Ministers' requirement for external testing, which was added to the normal NVQ-type continuous assessment. Not only was the resulting assessment system unmanageable, but teachers found themselves having to start the course without knowing what the assessment criteria were to be, and without sample test papers. When the first test papers did arrive there had been no time to put them through the usual process of piloting. Errors and anomalies were therefore discovered via the experiences of the first generation of students. (There are ominous echoes here of the situation with regard to the first generation of National Curriculum Tests.)

Even as late as 1995, the FEFC Inspectorate was reporting:

> *Many of the changes to assessment and grading practices which have occurred so far have resulted in only piecemeal improvements. The system remains too unwieldy to be either efficient or effective and further work is required.*
>
> (FEFC, 1995)

The same report was more positive about other aspects of GNVQs:

> *The quality of teaching and the promoting of learning is rising ... [though] ... after one or two years of operating GNVQs ... the quality of teaching on advanced GNVQs still compares unfavourably with that found on A level.*

> *Standards of work for students who are successful on Advanced GNVQs are broadly equivalent to those achieved by students on comparable vocational courses, or those achieved by students on GCE A levels studying two subjects.*

In other words, the Inspectors failed the *assessment/qualifications* regime, said that the *teaching/learning* programmes could be better, and gave a pass mark to the *standards* being achieved. It is important to distinguish between these three aspects of provision. The failure to take due account of each of these at the design stage of GNVQs contributed to the implementation difficulties. In effect, NCVQ issued a comprehensive set of standards by the deadline, as if these represented all that was required for quality provision. The design of an assessment regime to measure the achievement of the standards, and of learning programmes to enable students to reach the standards, had to follow. Not only did this not allow time for the assessment regime to be de-bugged, it did not provide for the standards to be amended in the light of insights gained through attempts to assess against them. Also, many teachers, particularly those in schools which had not offered the predecessor courses, needed much more guidance.

As Ofsted reported:

> *... some teachers ... found it difficult to devise programmes of learning which enabled their students to achieve all the outcomes required for the GNVQ, particularly in the newer areas of study; ...course design has been impeded by the continuing absence of clear guidance and insufficient exemplar materials... The average [time allocation] was 14 hours per week, but some allocations were as low as 4 hours per week, quite inadequate to cover the necessary work.*

> (Ofsted, 1994)

The problems were not all caused by the unrealistic schedule for implementation, but this certainly did not help. Some would argue that the fact that ministers agreed to and even required this rate of change was itself an illustration of the academic/vocational divide. It would never have been allowed for A levels.

It is instructive to compare the implementation schedule proposed by the Higginson Committee, whose proposals for A level reform were rejected by the government as being too radical. The proposals were made in 1988, subject groups were to have reported by early 1990, teacher training programmes should have been under development by mid-1990, and the new syllabuses were to be in use in schools and colleges by September 1992.

The GNVQ proposals were *really* radical, and were

- made by NCVQ in October 1991
- piloted in September 1992
- implemented in September 1993.

It is therefore not surprising that there followed:

- a six point 'agenda for action' to ensure rigour and quality set by Ministers in March 1994

- a fundamental review of GNVQ assessment under Dr John Capey in the Autumn of 1995 (Capey, 1995).

A classic case of 'more haste, less speed'!

The Dearing review of 16-19 qualifications

The remit given to Sir Ron by the Secretary of State in April 1995 was to advise on how to 'strengthen, consolidate and improve the framework of *16 to 19 qualifications.*' Cynics said that he was actually being asked to *devise* a framework for the three types of 'route' – A levels, NVQs and GNVQs – which had formed the basis of government policy since the 1991 White Paper. Within this overall task he was asked to 'ensure that the rigour and standards of GCE A levels are maintained' (Dearing, 1996a). The review took place in parallel with the Capey Review of GNVQs, and the Beaumont review of NVQs.

Continuing the 'route' metaphor, Dearing was being asked to create a more coherent road network whilst keeping the most elderly route unchanged, and whilst the two most recently designed were already under repair. Also, although the remit only made mention of three routes, a large number of students in the age group, and the majority of FE students, were taking qualifications which fell outside these routes. To his credit, Dearing went some way to recognising these issues. In his final Report, the first of his 198 recommendations is that there should be a National Framework of Qualifications, and he recognises that:

> there are legitimate claims that some of the existing (vocational) qualifications cater for needs that are not met either by an NVQ that required the candidate to have access to relevant employment, or by the broadly based GNVQ... The time is ripe for drawing these other qualifications into a more coherent framework that better meets the needs of candidates and employers.
>
> (Dearing, 1996b: para 6.20)

Dearing also made recommendations to do with improving the uniformity and clarity of A level standards. He argued that clarity could be improved through making the intended outcomes of A levels – that knowledge, understanding and skills a candidate would be expected to demonstrate for the award of a particular grade – more explicit.

Such a statement of outcomes is, of course, what is *meant* by the word 'standards' in the NVQ and GNVQ sense. We hit here one of the many differences of approach which bedevil our qualifications, and make it difficult to make them more coherent. When the then Secretary of State asked that 'A level standards should be maintained' she did not mean that, for instance, the learning outcomes of A level Physics should be the same now as they were in 1945, or as they should become by the year 2005.

She meant that – whatever the developments in the subject over time – its level of intellectual demand should remain equivalent.

In my view, Dearing only partially recognises the importance of clearing up some technical questions if his recommendation about a National Framework is to be effectively implemented – or even constructively debated.

For instance, if we were all to use the NCVQ definition of 'standards', it would allow people to argue for the maintenance of standards which make the same level of demand whilst querying the narrowness of a total programme for A level students which delivers these standards through the study of only three subjects. Seeing academic subjects as the primary *source* of these learning outcomes or standards, as opposed to the only means of delivering them, is extremely liberating, both to our thinking and to our timetabling.

Dearing recognises that clarity about the standards they embody is a strength of vocational qualifications, but in merely requiring that *'the (A level) regulatory bodies should examine the extent to which it is practical and advantageous to take further the specifications of A levels in terms of required learning outcomes'* (Dearing, 1996b: para 10.65) he underestimates the importance of this for the rest of what he wants.

For instance, he argues that the distinguishing characteristics of each of the three 'routes' should be made clear, and these should reflect their underlying purposes. As part of this he advocates that there should be identified *'broad principles for allocating subject areas to pathways'*. But *is* it the nature of a 'subject area' which distinguishes one pathway from another – or is it the nature of the learning outcomes (standards), or the learning programme, or the assessment method, or the purpose to which the qualification is put?

It is difficult to see how to decide whether 'economics' or even physics or English are academic or vocational in purpose, without comparing the intended learning outcomes of particular courses which have these titles. And how can these outcomes be compared if A levels do not state them, or if they state them in an idiosyncratic way which makes comparisons with other qualifications difficult?

At the same time as saying that the distinctiveness of each route should be preserved, Dearing argued for easier progression and transfer between them. This apparent paradox can be resolved as long as we are clear about whether their differences lie in:

- the nature of their intended learning outcomes (or standards)
- the source of the standards (e.g. the requirements of an academic subject, a vocational area, or a specific occupation)
- the structure of the learning programme
- the assessment regime.

This clarity cannot be achieved if outcomes are stated in different ways for no good reason, or are not stated at all, or if it is assumed that everything needs to be subject-based. It is not only Dearing who made this assumption about subjects. A linked report into the extent to which A levels and GNVQs can be taught together describes a GNVQ as being one 'subject', and suggests that an A level programme is broader because it contains three subjects (Coates & Hamilton, 1996). In fact, of course, two A level subjects may have overlapping outcomes (standards), and a single GNVQ may contain units which cover many different types of outcome.

Therefore we also need to make the necessary comparisons at the unit level, where a unit is a coherent group of outcomes. As the Scots and the New Zealanders are showing, it is possible to analyse academic as well as vocational qualifications into units, which clarifies rather than changes their distinctiveness. Analysis at unit level also helps to check that qualifications are equivalent in terms of the amount and level of achievement they require. As Dearing himself implies, this check is essential if other vocational qualifications and courses leading to Open College accreditation are also to be brought within the new framework.

In the end, Dearing fought shy of reference to *units*, probably because of political and practical concerns about *modularisation*. However, units describe what is being assessed in qualifications, and are relatively unproblematic, whereas modularisation is a method of structuring learning programmes which has risks as well as advantages.

This is an example of apparently simple proposals (about pathways, transfers and frameworks) being in reality technically problematic, whilst other approaches (making use of learning outcomes grouped into units) are avoided because of an overestimation of their difficulty.

Conclusions

While it is true that each of these initiatives had difficulties which were special to itself, there are others which they had in common, and which we are at risk of repeating. This risk arises not least because we have failed to identify the patterns in these developments.

Worse than this, we may be on the verge of misinterpreting the history. The myth being created is that the 'professionals' involved first produce an over-complex proposal, which is so difficult to implement that a pragmatic outsider has to be brought in to simplify matters in a common sense way. My thesis is that the difficulties are created by a combination of technical and managerial fallacies.

Because the 'pragmatic' approach of the various Capey, Beaumont and Dearing Reports of 1995/96 tends to avoid going back over the past, they have not identified the theoretical and policy assumptions which proved to have been dubious, and the managerial/political techniques which were unhelpful or obstructive. On the technical level, there has been a failure to understand the relationship between the necessary learning programmes, the learning outcomes (standards) being sought, and the qualifications required to test their achievement. With regard to the management of change, there has been a failure to use an identified development model, and to ensure that the right balance is kept between:

- curriculum development (meaning standards, qualifications and learning programmes)

- staff development (meaning skills, knowledge and understanding awareness)

- organisational development (meaning school and college structures, financial support, learning materials, record-keeping systems, and so on).

In policy terms, there has been a tendency to see each initiative in isolation from others, even though each could affect its success or failure of the rest: an unwillingness to think in terms of systems.

All of this has been overlaid by a fear of informed public debate, which has meant that crucial assumptions have not been examined and the impact of initiatives has been reported via assertions rather than in the form of more objective evaluations.

There are three things which could help make a reality of such a debate, and thus to make educational initiatives an ongoing part of a 'learning society', as opposed to a political football. These are:

a) a *shared language* in which to define achievement of all kinds, so that standards, learning programmes and qualifications can be compared and contrasted – not least for the benefit of the learners;

b) an open *forum for debate,* in which are represented those who need to influence standards, such as employers, unions and Universities, those who are responsible for assessment and certification (awarding and examining bodies), and those who are tasked to provide accessible, challenging and motivating learning programmes;

c) clarity about the appropriate *roles of the centre and the periphery.* In particular, we need government which resists the temptation to interfere with operational details, but accepts the responsibility for strategic management of the system as a whole and the boundaries between its constituent parts. It is in attempting to cross these boundaries that so many of our more vulnerable learners fall to the wayside.

Central government is increasingly and rightly requiring overt and good quality strategic planning and management from those it funds. Perhaps there should be a tax-payers' charter which demands the same from government with regard to the increasing number of central initiatives...

References

Association for Colleges (1996) *FE Now* March AfC

Beaumont G (1996) *Review of 100 NVQs and SVQs* NCVQ

Capey Dr J (1995) *Review of the assessment of GNVQs* NCVQ

City and Guilds of London Institute (1995) 'The Director General' in *C&G's Annual review, 1994–5* CGLI

Coates P & Hamilton J (1996) *16–19: coherence project review of 16–19 qualifications* Gatsby Foundation and SCAA

Dearing Sir Ron (1993a) *The National Curriculum and its assessment: interim report* July NCC/SEAC

Dearing Sir Ron (1993b) *The National Curriculum and its assessment: final report* December NCC/SEAC

Dearing Sir Ron (1996a) *Review of qualifications for 16–19 year olds* March SCAA

Dearing Sir Ron (1996b) *Review of qualifications for 16–19 year olds* Full report, section 16 SCAA

DeVille Sir Oscar (1986) *Review of vocational qualifications* April Manpower Services Commission/DES

Eggar T (1991a) in *DES Press Release* 21 March 1991

Eggar T (1991b) letter to Sir Bryan Nicholson (Chairman, NCVQ) DES May 1991

FEFC (1995) *General NVQs in further education sector in England* National Survey Report, FEFC Inspectorate

Graham D & Tytler D (1993) *A lesson for us all* Routledge

HMSO (1986) *White Paper Working together – education and training* HMSO

HMSO (1991) *White Paper: Education and training for the 21st century* HMSO

NCVQ/SCOTVEC (1996) *Review of 100 NVQs and SVQs: a report on the findings* NCVQ

OFSTED (1994) *GNVQs in schools, 1993/4* HMSO

Robinson P (1996) *NVQs: rhetoric and reality* Centre for Economic Performance, LSE

Robson J (1996) 'The New Zealand Qualifications Authority and the universities: progress towards a unified framework' *Journal of Vocational Education and Training* 46

13. The Employment Perspective
Stakeholders, Skills and Star-gazing: the Problematic Relationship between Education, Training and the Labour Market

Prue Huddlestone & Lorna Unwin

Introduction

This chapter will explore the relationship between post-16 education and training and the world of work and seek to define a research agenda within which issues related to that relationship can be raised and examined. Within post-16 education and training, further education colleges have always had a working relationship with industry and commerce and have their origins in the need for formal technical and vocational education at local and national levels. In other respects, however, significant elements of college life have become distanced from the world of work as these institutions have sought to gain academic respectability and, more recently, develop partnerships with higher education. A key question for all providers of post-16 education and training, and for this chapter, concerns the issue of balance of stakeholder interests. Can the current model of so-called employer-led post-16 education and training which is being promoted in the UK meet the needs of individuals as well as employers, and can employers themselves be supported by one vision of post-16 education and training given their diversity of scope, size and aspirations?

This chapter examines the extent to which post-16 education and training policies and practices are shaped by, reflect and adapt to the changing needs of the workplace and labour markets, and whether the concept of tripartism can usefully be employed to aid such an analysis. In writing this chapter, we have sought to take a multi-disciplinary approach drawing on our own work in the field of labour market studies, the employment-education interface, workplace training, and education and training policy making. We draw too on the research of economists and studies of the changing workplace. The research which informs the development of post-16 education and training and, in particular, vocational education and training (VET) comes from a range of disciplines which often do not have the language or inclination to speak to each other. For example, curriculum issues and qualifications' structures tend to be considered by educationalists in isolation from, say, economists' analyses of the labour market and business strategy. Hence we find that qualifications for both education and work are judged within an education paradigm and thus arguments about parity of esteem and the academic/vocational divide are based on the premise that vocational qualifications must prove themselves against an academic yardstick rather than being properly valued in their own right. Given the historic and continuing divisions which characterise post-16 education and training in England and Wales, it is important that research from the worlds of education, training and employment becomes more widely shared and assimilated.

Throughout the 1980s and 1990s, the discourse of post-16 education and training has been dominated by a recurring theme: the nation needs 'a highly skilled, flexible and motivated workforce' in order to cope with the 'impact of rapidly developing technologies, increasing international competition and industrial change' (DfEE, 1997). Under this rhetorical banner, a series of vocational education and training initiatives has been launched, the most recent of which, the Modern Apprenticeship, evokes the mythical workplace of an industrial golden age while at the same time claiming to provide a model of work-based post-16 education and training which is appropriate for the changing workplace of the future. Such interventions in the relationship between post-16 education and training and the world of work serve to strengthen and test that relationship whose many and diverse stakeholders have complex needs and goals.

This chapter is divided into three sections:

- Section One examines the relevance of traditional categories used to divide and separate members of the workforce in the light of the changing nature of the workplace itself and employment patterns at local, regional, national and international levels.

- Section Two examines the infrastructure of post-16 education and training and assesses the extent to which it is capable of responding to the needs of employment and, indeed, whether it is capable of helping to shape the world of work rather than simply acting in a passive provider role.

- Section Three discusses the ways in which both post-16 education and training and the world of work might develop their relationship given the pressures exerted on them from policy-makers and the world in general.

Tripartism, skills and the labour market

A significant indication that tripartism may be an appropriate form of categorisation when describing the world of work is the concern surrounding this country's supposedly poor performance in terms of 'intermediate skills', a term which embraces 'craft' as well as 'technician' skills. While accepting such definitions are necessarily imprecise at the boundaries, Ryan (1992) describes intermediate skills as 'those above routine skills but below professional ones' and sees them as being characterised by three distinctive attributes:

> *Firstly, such skills are costly to develop, which marks them off from routine skills. Secondly, they are – or could readily become – highly transferable across employers which marks them off from employer-specific skills, however costly. Thirdly, in Britain they have traditionally been developed predominantly through workplace-based training programmes such as apprenticeship which marks them off from professional skills.*

(Ryan, 1992: 2–3)

Several research studies in the 1980s and early 1990s highlighted Britain's historic failure to develop adequate supplies of intermediate skills in comparison with its economic competitors, notably France and Germany (in particular: Prais, 1981; Finegold & Soskice, 1988; Steedman, 1988; Steedman *et al.* 1991). The identification of a problem at the level of intermediate skills presupposes that the labour market and employer demand for certain types of labour are stratified along tripartite lines: *unskilled, skilled* (craft/technician), *professional*. Just as the British education system was structured to reflect Plato's tripartite division of society, so the workplace could be said to divide itself into three categories of employee. The failure by employers to expand and develop the workforce's middle tier (those using intermediate skills), which itself divides into skilled and semi-skilled, was mirrored by the failure of successive governments to develop an adequate system of technical education and, until very recently, in the low numbers of young people participating in education beyond the age of 16 compared to most other industrialised nations.

Historically, Britain's 'skilled' workforce was developed through the apprenticeship system which, through the central role of trade unions, imposed job demarcations in industry and limited training opportunities for non-apprenticed workers (Keep & Mayhew, 1994). In manufacturing industry, three categories of employee – *unskilled, semi-skilled* and *skilled* – formed the basis on which wage rates were determined for hourly paid workers (blue-collar) as opposed to salaried staff (white-collar) (see Ainley, 1993). Yet, as Ainley ... reminds us, tripartism in the education system and in the workplace may have more to do with concepts of social class than they have with clear definitions of what constitutes the nature and content of different skills. Ainley quotes Gallie, who noted that there is:

> ... *little consensus between analysts about what constitutes skill or how it can be measured. The very complexity of the task of defining skill makes it implausible that skill classifications in industry reflect in an unproblematic way some objective hierarchy. Rather, they are likely to be the product of a continuous negotiation between employers and employees, in which both relative power resources and prevalent cultural beliefs will influence the grading structure.*
>
> (Gallie, 1988: 7–8)

Here Gallie is referring to occupational skills, that is those skills which constitute particular job-specific tasks, but to these we must also add the even more vaguely defined *social skills* (also referred to as *generic, personal, transferable, core* and, since the 1996 Dearing Review, *key* skills) which are thought to underpin all workplace activity (as well as that outside the workplace). Green (1996: 22) draws our attention to emerging literature which suggests that 'much of what goes under the name of training is not just to raise the technical skills of the workforce but also to improve their "social skills"'. These social skills include 'qualities and behavioural norms that arise in response to the conflictual relation between boss and worker, and which are valued by employers' (ibid). Getting to know and understand how to behave in the workplace, to imbibe specific workplace cultures and to be socialised sufficiently to ensure one's face fits are stages through which every employee has to pass.

In the late 1970s and early 1980s, such stages and their accompanying skills came to be gradually defined in curriculum terms and incorporated into the emerging youth training schemes devised by the Manpower Services Commission (MSC). The underlying objective of what became known as the 'new vocationalism' was to try and make young people (and to some extent unemployed adults) more acceptable to employers who, it was said, could not fill their vacancies because they could not find enough people with the right skills and attitudes (Finn, 1987). As Wellington (1993) and others have shown, however, in addition to the fact that employers do not form a unitary category in themselves, their demands should not be allowed to dominate national systems of education and training, for the following reasons:

- the needs of employers may not coincide with the needs of the nation

- employers may be unaware that their professed needs are not actually in the interest of their own organisations

- concepts such as *qualities and attributes* may be confused with specific skills

- recruitment and selection practices do not always relate to the skills and attributes employers say they require.

While it is clear that employers differ enormously in terms of their human resource requirements, and that each organisation reflects what Fevre (1992) refers to as 'industrial values' in terms of the way in which employer and employee relate to and treat each other, it is also clear that employers do have a justifiable right to expect the education system to provide people with enough basic skills (literacy and numeracy in particular) on which they can build. Unfortunately, a key problem for the British economy has been and continues to be a tendency by significant numbers of large and small employers to expect the education system to provide all the education and training enabling them to absorb all the benefits without having to share any of the costs (Keep & Mayhew, 1994).

We now wish to return to the point made earlier that employers have a right to expect that potential employees will have achieved a general level of basic education. Given the changing nature of most workplaces and the increase in jobs which require multiple skills, gaining access to much of the job market (and certainly the legitimate job market as opposed to informal, unregulated areas) means a more competitive environment in which qualification credentialism is rampant. For young people, and particularly those who choose to leave compulsory schooling at the earliest opportunity, trying to enter today's labour market will seem a particularly demanding and daunting prospect.

The youth labour market, as Ashton (1993) reminds us, has some distinctive features but it is subject to 'the forces of change which operate on adult labour markets' and so in order to understand how the youth labour market might be evolving we need to understand the forces of change affecting its adult counterpart. Ashton identifies the key features which are affecting labour markets throughout the industrialised world and which we summarise as follows:

- the growth of multi-national corporations and the decline in the control which national governments can have over their economies

- the emergence of transnational and regionalised trading blocs which create new ways of integrating capital and labour

- changes in the method of organising production within companies which are increasing the importance of internal labour markets and stressing the need for flatter organisational structures in which employees are required to work flexibly

- the chosen role of the business elite – such elites can operate autonomously from governments and choose to buck the trends in organisational change referred to above, hence they might choose to operate their businesses with a predominantly low-skilled workforce and use new technology to de-skill tasks

- the chosen role of the national political elite – some governments, such as Singapore and Taiwan, are pursuing an industrial strategy based on high skills and have developed their education and training systems accordingly whereas the UK and the USA have concentrated on removing barriers to market forces and let education continue to reflect the *status quo*.

In Britain, industrial strategy (and the absence of it) has been characterised by the craft apprenticeships which operated completely separately from government and state-sponsored youth training. From the late 1970s until the launch of the Modern Apprenticeship in 1994, government sponsored training concentrated on the development of low skills (Levels 1 and 2) from which only half the number of trainees who participate emerge with a vocational qualification. Under Ashton's analysis, young people in the Pacific Rim will find that the 'main demand for their labour will be in jobs which demand a high level of conceptual and social skills as well as technical knowledge and which offer the prospect of continuous learning', whereas in Britain young people may find 'their future employment prospects confined to the external labour market in low paid, semi-skilled jobs interspersed with periods of unemployment' (Ashton, 1993: 21).

Increasing industrial and commercial globalisation, the impact of new technologies, the growth of the personal services sector, and the decline of mass manufacturing have clearly affected patterns of working, recruitment and training in industry and commerce (Llewellyn, 1996). Gilbert (1996) notes that recent empirical work on the introduction of new technology challenges the deterministic analysis of what he calls the 'old industrial sociology' that employers will tend to use technology to de-skill and control employees (Ashton above) but stresses that employers need to learn how to create and use new organisational techniques. The 1995 Annual Employment Survey revealed that 75% of employees are now in the service sector and 18% in manufacturing (Roberts *et al.* 1996) and it is forecast that any increase in jobs in manufacturing and related industries will be of a professional, managerial or technical nature (DfEE, 1997). While such star-gazing may prove to be accurate, the reality of many workplaces still presents a different picture and one in which the production lines, hierarchical structures and culture which characterised the so-called Fordist manufacturing companies are still in place. Moves to a post-Fordist world of work across the board would seem to be exaggerated (Keep & Mayhew, 1994). Although there are sectors of the economy which are dependent upon high level skills and investment in new technologies, Britain occupies a particular niche in the international division of labour, whereby some of its major industrial sectors are based on low value-added mass production processes, producing relatively low quality goods (Marginson, 1994). In addition, youth unemployment remains high so the numbers of disaffected young people grow posing problems for education and training systems which seek to provide opportunities beyond compulsory schooling (Istance *et al.* 1994). Added to this, the traditional patterns of recruitment which define the internal and external labour market continue to operate.

Employment variations between regions and localities should not be overlooked ... and support the view that education and training providers must be responsive to and aware of the nature and scope of the communities they seek to serve. For example, comparative research by Cockrill, Scott & Fitz (1996) on multi-skilling in Britain and Germany describes the very localised nature of the South Wales labour market as follows: recruitment tends to be restricted to the local area; some employers look to past employees as their first source of new recruits; people want to work where they live and so have little incentive to restrict their skills to one occupation; and people work wherever positions are available locally and in whichever firm offers the best conditions. Cockrill *et al.* state that:

> *For many workers, it does not seem to matter much whether they work as a machine operator, supermarket shelver or as a skilled engineer as long as it is local and the pay is not too bad.*

> (Cockrill *et al.* 1996: 4)

Inequalities of access to and provision of employment and training based on class, gender and ethnicity can be clearly seen in labour market statistics, and challenge the positive view of flexibility as envisaged in *flexible specialisation, flexible firms* and the *flexible labour market*. (For critiques of the concept of flexible specialisation, see Pollert 1988, and Fielder, 1992.) And, nationally, those statistics show that where there has been a growth in employment, it has been in part-time, temporary employment. Figures show that 27.5% of employees in 1995 were in part-time work (LMT November, 1996). The government estimates that, between 1983 and 1994, some 1.9 million part-time jobs were created, a significant number of which were taken by women (DTI *et al.* 1996). An IES report (Atkinson *et al.* 1995) confirms this trend pointing to the growth in part-time employment across all sectors. Of those employers interviewed for the report, 40% stated that their main reason for employing temporary staff was 'to match staff levels to peaks in demand'. It is also known that such employees have less access to training than permanent employees and that employers saw the need to train temporary workers as a particular disadvantage, possibly one which they would seek to avoid.

Part-time jobs are also, of course, taken by young people who are officially registered as being in full-time education. In their research, Atkinson *et al.* (1996) revealed that the highest proportion of temporary workers (18%) was in the 16–19 age group. Recent work by Unwin (1995) showed that significant numbers of full-time students between 16 and 18 in Cheshire were working an average of 15 hours per week: at weekends, in the evening, and in their free periods. (National data from the Youth Cohort Study shows that 47% of students work between 5 and 10 hours, 28% between 10 and 20 hours, and 5% over 20 hours.) The extension of Sunday trading and increase in temporary work have created more jobs for students. Hourly payment of, in some cases, up to £4 per hour; means that young people can earn twice the weekly youth training allowance (£29.50 for a 16-year-old) by working two shifts in a supermarket. In the Cheshire sample, college students described how the concentration of assignments on GNVQ courses into two or three weeks in a term, meant they could work very hard in short bursts and then use their free study days to sign up for temporary work in local factories. Despite being classed as full-time students, these young people were working as many hours in paid employment as they were spending in an educational institution. The challenge this poses to curriculum planners and to the qualifications system is how can this part-time activity be integrated into a more holistic approach to post-16 education and training and, if possible, how can it be accredited? It may be that young people are acquiring Dearing's so-called *key skills* as well as occupational skills in their part-time working life.

Given the complex and changing realities of the labour market and the workplace, tripartite categorisations are evidently far too simplistic, for not only do they impose clarity on an unclear world but they also imply a rigidity which negates the fluidity of skills and the ability of people to move position within and across organisations. Yet the shadow of tripartism is still cast across policy documents which classify occupational sectors and jobs and education and training policies which separate people into the unskilled, skilled and professional.

Merson (1996) draws our attention to the emphasis in current Government policy in relation to the labour market on the need to promote flexibility of conditions for immediate economic gain. He suggests that less attention is given to longer-term investment in the development of skills. The current rhetoric rarely addresses the social implications of flexibility of conditions and the attendant uncertainties of short-term contracts, temporary employment and financial insecurity. While it is generally recognised that many people in the future will have a number of job/career changes and may have to re-train several times, there will be others who will move in and out of casual employment or who will spend some of their working life in the informal economy.

The structure of post-16 education and training

The history of voluntarism which has allowed employers in the UK to opt in or out of investing in workforce training, as and when they choose, has been well-documented (Finegold & Soskice, 1988, *inter alia*). Despite this knowledge, however, the Government and its related agencies proclaim that vocational education and training is now *employer-led*. Such rhetoric gives succour to the belief that the following have been created by and are being further developed with the active involvement of employers:

- National Vocational Qualifications (NVQs)
- Training and Enterprise Councils (TECs)
- Education-business partnerships (EBPs).

That employers have singularly failed to show enthusiasm for NVQs (Robinson, 1996), regard TECs at best as potential sources of funding and at worst as interfering bureaucracies (Unwin, 1994), and have a varied response to EBPs whose performance is patchy (IES, 1995), betrays the shallowness of the concept of an *employer-led* vocational education and training system. We need to separate the reality of the relationship between education, training and the world of work from what Coffield has referred to as the 'farrago of hurrah words' in which discourse, innumerable White Papers and so-called *consultative* documents have been written in the last twenty or so years (Coffield, 1990). Employers are involved in post-16 education and training in many and different ways. At local level, some employers act as governors of colleges, directors of TEC boards and members of Chambers of Commerce. At national level, they might represent their sector's interests on the boards of Industrial Training Organisations (ITOs) or the Lead Bodies which define standards of competence. But most employers interact with the post-16 education and training system as consumers and providers and know little of the way in which its policies and practices are formulated. If evidence from Raper *et al.* (1997), which suggests that more and more companies are satisfying their training needs in-house and recognising the workplace as a site for learning, is indicative of a growing trend then the relationship between employers and the post-16 education and training system may become even more tenuous, perhaps only really active at the recruitment stage or through involvement with state-sponsored schemes.

Given the constant intervention by Government in the youth labour market since the late 1970s, it is difficult to assess the extent to which employers can be said to be still in a leading role. Employers could be said to have acquiesced in the creation of a publicly funded and state-constructed youth labour market which has provided training (sometimes of a dubious nature) but not lasting employment for young people. (For a critique of youth training schemes see in particular, Ainley & Corney, 1990, and Coles, 1995.) Clearly employers have a leading role in that they can choose to offer or withhold jobs and training places but once the Government chose to subsidise youth training and, subsequently, to guarantee all school leavers a training place (removing at the same time the right of 16 to 19-year-olds to claim unemployment benefit) they caused a subtle shift in the employers' role. In order to meet what became known as the 'youth training guarantee' and to counteract market failure in terms of youth employment by intervening directly in the youth labour market, the government charged its locally-based agencies (now the Training and Enterprise Councils) with signing up employers to the national youth project. Without the subsidies and the inducements to play a part in helping the nation meet its national education and training targets, the youth labour market might have a very different appearance. The following questions are, therefore, pertinent:

1) How many of the 263,500 young people currently on Youth Training (Roberts *et al.* 1996) have employed status and a real chance of their employment continuing beyond the point when the YT funding ends?

2) How many of the 60,000 people on Modern Apprenticeship (LMT, March 1995) are in placements converted from YT rather than on apprenticeships newly created by the employers themselves?

3) How many of the estimated 90,000 young people not officially recorded as being in full-time education or on a government-sponsored training scheme are working in the informal labour market?

TECs, like their educational neighbours, are chasing young people in order to meet the difficult targets they are set each year by the Government Regional Offices working on behalf of the DfEE. This competitive market impels TECs to manipulate the labour market. Through-puts are more important than attention to local and regional planning related to skills shortages and future skill needs, hence newspaper headlines about the thousands of hairdressers being trained at the public's expense. Large companies also benefit, however, from the TECs' need to meet their YT and Modern Apprenticeship targets and one wonders how far the UK's car industry is currently benefiting from the Treasury's decision to turn a blind eye to the issue of *deadweight training* funding, that is the payment of subsidies for training which employers would normally fund themselves.

The poor image of YT has seen recruitment to that scheme fall consistently during the 1990s, while, at the same time, the contraction of the youth labour market, introduction of GNVQs and a concerted campaign by schools and colleges to persuade young people to remain in full-time education (71% nationally now stay on) have created a sea-change in post-16 destination patterns. Here again, however, one needs to stress the distorting effect of competitive funding regimes. Despite the celebration of that much improved staying-on figure, we know that between 30 and 40% of young people do not complete their post-16 courses (Audit Commission, 1993). Research has shown that some young people are persuaded, contrary to their own wishes, to remain in full-time education by their teachers, that some drift into staying-on because it feels safe and as a result of peer pressure, and that some have no choice due to poor labour market opportunities.

Work currently being undertaken by Huddleston in West Midlands' colleges has highlighted a new cohort of young people, those pursuing one year GNVQ Intermediate programmes. These young people are proving difficult to teach since they are using college as a 'parking place' because of the lack of jobs. Their chosen programme of study often bears little relationship to their future employment plans, or indeed to any plans at all. Research on destination patterns in Derbyshire between 1990 and 1993 also showed that significant numbers of young people had drifted into staying on in full-time education rather than making a definite decision to do so (Fergusson & Unwin, 1996). Regional differences should also be noted here, both in terms of the nature and extent of post-16 participation and achievement rates. Figures for the percentage of young people gaining a qualification (or units towards a full NVQ) at the end of their YT programme, for example, show that on Merseyside as few as 36% achieve this compared to 74% in Suffolk (Roberts *et al.* 1996).

In January 1997, the figure for employees receiving any kind of training at work (both on and off-the-job) was just over 14% (LMT, January 1997), a figure that has hardly changed since 1989. Government training statistics (DfEE, 1996) indicate that the majority of employer-based training is delivered to meet statutory requirements (for example, *Health and Safety* regulations) rather than for more broadly-based developmental reasons. In addition, those who already hold qualifications are more likely to gain access to further qualifications and those in professional and managerial occupations are more likely to receive training than those in lower level occupations.

Comments from a Training Agency survey of company attitudes to trainer training noted how this antipathy to investment in training has been translated into lack of status for the trainers themselves:

> *Many of the companies participating in this survey reported that there were difficulties in providing a satisfactory career structure for specialist 'career trainers' because of the small size of the training departments involved... More generally, companies seeking to make use of 'non-career trainers', while on secondment, also need to ensure that the training department is not perceived by potential recruits as a 'dead end' which removes other career options.*
>
> (Training Agency, 1990a: 41)

As Bennett & McCoshan (1993) note, management training in Britain is also poor in comparison to other countries and, significantly, training does not generally figure when companies develop their business plans. An Industrial Society survey of 500 companies in 1991 showed that only 16% built training into their business plans.

This British ambivalence towards training has deep roots. As Ainley & Corney (1990) and Vlaeminke (1990) have indicated, Britain managed a sustained industrial revolution without any formal training policy or provision, so it is perhaps not surprising that repeated warnings about a potential skills' deficit in Britain have never been treated with the seriousness they deserve.

Qualifications and the labour market

If tripartism has been found to be too simplistic as a concept for describing the world of work (and the way in which people divide as learners ...), it does appear more plausible when applied to the current structure of qualifications on offer to learners in the post-16 education and training phase.

At first glance, the qualifications framework divides into two: the academic (GCSEs, A levels, degrees) and the vocational (GNVQs, NVQs, and vocational awards which lie outside the NVQ framework). The vocational pathway, however, could now be said to split as GNVQs, which have provided access to higher education, straddle the academic-vocational divide thus forming a middle band and creating a tripartite structure... It is worth noting here that, according to recent research by Robinson (1997), the old academic-vocational dualism appears still to apply in the labour market even if in colleges and schools the post-16 education and training curriculum presents a tripartite image. [However], Robinson presents the post-16 education and training qualifications structure as a straightforward dualism and states:

> *There can be no parity of esteem in education and training between academic and vocational qualifications because there is no parity of esteem in the labour market where academic qualifications tend to offer access to more highly paid occupations and often pay a higher wage within those occupations than their*

nationally equivalent vocational counterparts. This is true at all levels of the national qualifications framework.

(Robinson, 1997: 3)

Robinson's analysis, which is set against the five-level framework used in the National Education and Training Targets, suggests that people with academic qualifications at one level earn about the same as people with vocational qualifications set at one level higher. This means, for example, that people with A levels (Level 3) earn the same as those with vocational qualifications at Level 4 and those with five or more GCSEs at Grades A–C (Level 2) earn the same as those with Level 3 vocational qualifications. While qualifications are not designed with pay in mind, the differential levels of reward in terms of pay, status, and promotional prospects give out powerful signals to those pursuing different qualifications. Employers may also have fixed views about the most desirable qualifications for recruits, even to the extent that recruits may well be over-qualified for the jobs to which they have been recruited. As well as implying a fundamental flaw in the levels set for the qualifications framework, Robinson's analysis also challenges Dearing's assertion that his proposed national framework of awards will have 'the important purpose of making plain that academic, applied and vocational qualifications are of equal value' (Dearing, 1996: 14).

Research by Unwin & Wellington (1995) into the reasons why young people were attracted to the pilot year of Modern Apprenticeship showed that although they had chosen a work-based route as opposed to remaining in full-time education, these new apprentices still had academic qualifications in their sights. Significant numbers spoke of their desire to gain a university degree at some point and saw the apprenticeship as a route to such a qualification hopefully sponsored by their employer. Others hoped to gain extra GCSEs alongside their vocational qualifications, particularly in subjects such as foreign languages or mathematics which might be useful in the workplace. It is a testament to the lack of vision that has bedevilled youth training schemes that little attempt has been made to create programmes which combine the opportunity to learn job-specific skills, to which many young people are attracted, as well as continuing with an academic education (see Evans *et al.* 1997). Some of the occupational sectors associated with the Modern Apprenticeship, notably in engineering, chemicals and the steel industry, are showing that employers, working together with colleges, want to develop a sufficiently broad-based training experience that embraces the academic as well as the vocational. (This is discussed in more detail below.)

In his analysis of the performance of NVQs, Robinson (1996) found that they have been largely concentrated in the personal service, clerical and sales sectors as opposed to the manufacturing and business and financial services sectors. He also found NVQs to be under-represented in the higher managerial, professional and technical occupations and that, overall, there was no evidence to suggest that the introduction of NVQs had increased the amount of training available to individuals. NVQs, of course, were designed to be specifically related to the world of work rather than of education but the first three NVQ levels reflect the perception of the traditional workplace (operatives, technicians/supervisors, managers) held by the world of education. This in turn enshrines the notion of hierarchical and fixed competences which may conflict with the flat structures of the changing modern workplace. The now extensive critique of NVQs points to their many flaws but for this chapter, two in particular stand out:

1. NVQs at Levels 1 and 2 offer a very limited and basic VET menu for young people in comparison to VET programmes in other countries, and even at Level 3, providers have to find ways of covering the necessary underpinning knowledge by turning to other qualifications, notably BTEC National and GNVQ units.

2. NVQs fail to meet employers' needs, either because they are inflexible or because they are not specific enough – whichever way, NVQs are decidedly not employer-led.

Whether it is deemed to be dualistic or tripartite, how appropriate then is the current post-16 education and training qualifications framework to the world of work? The inappropriateness of its divisions and rigidity is perhaps well-illustrated in the Modern Apprenticeship (MA) where young people can often be found studying for a range of qualifications as none alone appears to be quite right. The MA is based on training frameworks which are developed by Industrial Training Organisations (ITOs) in conjunction with TECs. It is open to young people between the ages of 16 and 24. Funding is tied to TEC outcomes and hence the MA is tied to NVQs. Apprentices have to work towards a minimum NVQ Level 3, but this is supplemented by GNVQ Key Skill units and other GNVQ units to provide underpinning knowledge. Some employers have also insisted that their apprentices study for the traditional BTEC National qualification which now lies outside the NVQ framework, and some include GCSEs in Modern Languages.

While some MA schemes are highly selective (requiring four or more GCSEs at Grades A–C), many are not. Apprentices can begin their training with the Level 2 NVQ and progress to the Level 3 but this will not improve their standard of general education (gaining, for example, Maths and English at GCSE),which provides the all-important measure of ability most employers would expect when recruiting people they want to train for the future. Young people on the Youth Training Scheme are funded to NVQ Level 2 and statistics show that only half of YT trainees actually complete their qualification.

Adults are particularly ill-served by the current qualifications structure. They will find it difficult to access GCSE and A level classes other than in the evening and in some parts of the country such provision will either be at a very high cost or not exist at all. They may gain access to NVQs and other vocational qualifications in the workplace, but, according to research from the National Institute for Adult Continuing Education (NIACE), the majority of adults gaining qualifications will be in full-time rather than part-time work, will be in the higher social class bands and will have stayed in full-time education until the age of 18 (NIACE, 1994).

The unemployed may access NVQs if they participate in a government-sponsored scheme such as Training for Work but achievement levels are similar to those found on youth training in that they hover at just under 50% annually. In terms of studying for both academic and vocational qualifications, NIACE found that the majority of adults were doing so for labour market reasons and, regardless of whether they were in work, the majority had had to find the funding themselves.

The problems adults face are particularly ironic in the light of the Government's current preoccupation with lifelong learning. Individuals are being exhorted to become lifelong learners, to develop skills of flexibility and to enhance their personal skills but these may be exactly the luxuries for which employers do not wish to pay. If 'learning pays' who is going to fund the initial investment? For many, the answer is the individual must pay unless he or she is lucky enough to have found employment with an employer willing to make such an investment. Small and medium-sized enterprises may lack both the means and the inclination to be so forward-looking (Huddleston, 1996).

In terms of the National Education and Training Targets, those employers who do want to recruit people with an adequate level of general education on which to build substantive occupational or multi-skilled training have cause to be concerned. Nationally, just under two thirds of young people gain five GCSEs at grades A–C but only one quarter gain such grades in Maths and English. At local level, the figures differ enormously. In Sheffield, for example, the figures for five GCSEs grades A–C drop to 42% and, in some schools, can be as low as 1%.

Given the inadequacies of NVQs, how will the National Target of 85% of 19 to 21-year-olds achieving the Level 2 threshold by the year 2000 (whether at GCSE, GNVQ Intermediate or NVQ) be reached? And even if it is reached, will the fact that some young people will have only got there by virtue of NVQs be a cause for celebration?

The way forward

How best then is the post-16 education and training system to serve the needs of such a future workforce, and, as importantly, future citizens? This chapter has tried to show how difficult it is to predict with certainty the ways in which work patterns, labour market demand and the economic climate in general will evolve over time. It does seem certain, however, that tripartite notions of how workplaces divide in terms of tasks and employee capability are far too simplistic. Although employers have been shown to send out very confused messages when discussing the types of skills they need from their current and future workforce, they do reveal in their recruitment and human resource management behaviour that they value academic qualifications as highly, and in some cases more highly than vocational ones. In order to meet the challenges of running a business in the new century, most employers will expect their workforce to have an adequate level of general education on which they can build through specific job-related training.

Given that employers will tend to train for their immediate needs and have a preference for skills which are only specific to their organisations (Huddleston & Rainbird, 1996), the post-16 education and training system has to find ways to meet both the employers' needs and those of the individual. For young people, the balance is particularly important. Gleeson (1996) warns against using 'economic rationalism' to drive education and the managerialist paradigm within which teachers and learners are being forced to live:

> *Here, preoccupation with improved participation, qualification and skills, though ostensibly to do with improved productivity and employment, has little to do with enabling young people to think critically about themselves, their community and society.*

(Gleeson, 1996: 97)

It may be the case that creative application of and greater equity of access to the new technologies will revolutionise working life and leisure though, as Aronowitz & DiFazio (1994) stress, naiveté is highly dangerous in this respect. What is needed is a re-examination of the relationship between work, society and people's lives. Education and employment have a great deal to learn about each other's purposes, structures, cultures and developing patterns of behaviour. The concept of *training,* as opposed to *education,* deserves fresh attention for it seems to us that it has got lost in the murky waters of Government-sponsored schemes of social engineering and has become too narrowly defined through the introduction of competence-based models of skill acquisition. One way forward would be to develop what might be termed a *pedagogy of work* in which research about how people learn in both the academic and vocational spheres can be harnessed (Fuller & Unwin, 1996).

The current education-based qualification paradigm is linked closely to the professions and higher education, but misses the general world of work. In the middle (the general world of work), at the heart of the post-16 education and training system, sit FE colleges which need to assert their ability to provide education and training for the majority of workplaces, albeit with the expertise to offer professional qualifications as well. But FE needs to reclaim the vocational and technical curriculum and have the authority to respond to the needs of local, regional and national employers.

Two barriers exist which prevent FE colleges from responding adequately to this general world of work. Firstly, the FEFC funding methodology does not provide any particular incentive for this as it simply requires colleges to increase student numbers. The easiest way to do this is to offer popular courses. One example here is the current popularity of GNVQ Leisure and Tourism programmes which attract students, and hence funding, but which do not, necessarily, lead to jobs. Secondly, to respond adequately and plan to meet labour market need, colleges require sophisticated labour market information. TECs have a remit to collect such information but they differ in terms of their capability to do so, as do local authority research units. Since FE sector incorporation in 1993, colleges have been released from local authority control and are in competition with TECs (who have set targets to reach for their YT and Modern Apprenticeship places) for young people. Bringing these different stakeholders together (colleges, TECs and local authorities) is time-consuming and often relies on the determined efforts of enthusiastic individuals. As such, it is no wonder that labour market planning lacks coherence and a substantive research base at local and regional level.

Without that underpinning labour market knowledge and understanding, there is a potential mismatch between the qualifications offered by FE and the opportunities in the labour market. Perhaps even more worryingly, at national level, the relationship between Government-sponsored training schemes and labour market needs is at best on nodding acquaintance. The DfEE has recently commissioned a research study to investigate the potential coverage by the Modern Apprenticeship of all occupational sectors which themselves are covered by NVQs up to Level 3. In its specification for the research, the DfEE listed a number of databases which could be interrogated to try and construct a meaningful picture of the youth labour market while, at the same time, admitting that these databases were seriously flawed.

A similar problem exists in attempting to assess the take-up and coverage of NVQs (Huddleston *et al.* 1996). The major problem still remains the lack of reliable quantitative data concerning the take-up of NVQs by sector, level, candidate profile and geographical distribution. The differing methods of data collection used by the different awarding bodies, providers and government agencies make true comparisons impossible.

FE colleges are in an ideal position to act as a bridge between education and work but are also under pressure to worship before the academic altar and compete for students with schools, sixth form colleges and higher education institutions. By working with their industrial and business partners and other post-16 education and training providers, colleges could develop research-led learning and skills maps of their communities and of specialist industries with which they already work. This could form part of a sub-regional/local economic development strategy and FE Competitiveness Fund bids might usefully be focused along these lines. TECs are charged with the responsibility for collecting labour market and other relevant information to measure progress towards NTETs. Although, admittedly, some of this is patchy, it is potentially valuable for colleges in developing their own strategic plans (CEI, 1997). Such research would, in turn, help us learn more about when, how and if people divide along tripartite, dualistic or other lines and whether such divisions are worth maintaining as a basis on which to construct a system of education and training.

References

Ainley P & Corney M (1990) *Training for the future, the rise and fall of the Manpower Services Commission* Cassell

Ainley P (1993) *Class and skill* Cassell

Aronowitz S & DiFazio W (1994) *The jobless future: sci-tech and the dogma of work* University of Minnesota Press

Ashton D (1993) 'Understanding change in youth labour markets: a conceptual framework' *British Journal of Education & Work* 6 (3)

Atkinson J *et al.* (1996) *Temporary work and the labour market* Institute for Employment Studies: Report no 311

Audit Commission/Ofsted (1993) *Unfinished business* Stationery Office

Bennett R & McCoshan A (1993) *Enterprise and human resource development* Paul Chapman

CEI (1997) *The role of education in economic development* A National Development Project funded by DfEE, University of Warwick, Centre for Education and Industry

Cockrill A, Scott P & Fitz J (1996) *Training for multi-skilling: a comparison of British and German experience* (Paper at 1996 BERA Conference, Lancaster University)

Coffield F (1990) 'From the decade of enterprise to the decade of TECs' *British Journal of Education and Work* 4 (1) pp58–78

Coles B (1995) *Youth and social policy* UCL Press

Dearing R (1996) *Review of qualifications for 16–19 year olds* SCAA

DfEE (1996) *Training statistics 1996* Stationery Office

DfEE (1997) *Meeting the challenge of the 21st century, a summary of labour market and skill trends 1997–98* Skills and Enterprise Network, Department for Education and Employment

DTI *et al.* (1995) *Competitiveness: helping business to win* Cm.2867 Stationery Office

DTI *et al.* (1996) *Competitiveness, forging ahead* Stationery Office

Evans K *et al.* (1997) 'Working to learn: a work-based route to learning for young people' *Issues in People Management* 18 Institute of Personnel and Development

Fergusson R & Unwin L (1996) *Making better sense of post-16 destinations: a case study of an English shire county* Research Papers in Education 1 (1)

Fevre R (1992) *The sociology of labour markets* Harvester Wheatsheaf

Fielder S (1992) 'Recruitment, training and local economic restructuring: an analysis' *British Journal of Education and Work* 5 (2)

Finegold D & Soskice D (1988) 'The failure of training in Britain: analysis and prescription' *Oxford Review of Economic Policy* 4 (3)

Finn D (1987) *Training without jobs* Macmillan

Fuller A & Unwin L (1996) *Reconceptualising apprenticeship: exploring the relationship between work and learning* Paper presented to the inaugural conference of the Work and Learning Network, November 14th, University of Sheffield

Gallie D (1988) *Employment in Britain* Blackwell

Gilbert M (1996) 'New technology: old industrial sociology?' *New Technology, Work and Employment* 11 (1)

Gleeson D (1996) Post-compulsory education in a post-industrial and post-modern age in J Avis *et al.* (eds) *Knowledge and nationhood* Cassell Education

Green F (1996) *Skill, training, organisational commitment and employment: the economics of a labour management strategy* Discussion Paper No 313 Centre for Economic Performance, LSE

Hillage J, Hyndley K & Pike G (1995) *Employers' views of education business links* Institute for Employment Studies

Huddleston P (1996) *In what ways can VET systems meet the needs of old and new market economies? More questions than answers* Paper presented to the International Seminar on Training in the Market Economy, National Institute for Vocational Education, Budapest, Hungary

Huddleston P & Rainbird H (1996) 'Les relations centre travaille et curriculum en Angleterre et au Pays de Galles: reconstruction ou demolition?' *La Revue des sciences de l'education* XXI (4) Quebec

Huddleston P, Carey S & Johnston C (1996) *Marketing NVQs: a study of the operating environment final report* Centre for Education and Industry, University of Warwick

IRS (1994) 'Recruiting and training school leavers' IRS *Employee Development Bulletin* 54

Istance D, Rees G & Williamson H (1994) *Young people not in education, training or employment in South Glamorgan* South Glamorgan Training and Enterprise Council

Keep E & Mayhew K (1994) 'UK training policy – assumptions and reality' in A Booth & DJ Snower (eds) *The skills gap and economic activity* Cambridge University Press

Llewellyn J (1996) 'Tackling Europe's competitiveness' *Oxford Review of Economic Policy* 12 (3)

LMT (1995) 'Inter-TEC comparisons, 1994–95' *Labour Market Trends* November Stationery Office, pp63–80

LMT (1997) 'Labour force survey' *Labour Market Trends* March Stationery Office

Marginson P (1994) 'Multinational Britain: employment and work in an international economy' *Human Resource Management Journal* 4 (4)

Merson M (1996) 'Education, training and the flexible labour market' *British Journal of Education and Work* 9 (2)

NIACE (1994) *What price the learning society?* National Institute for Adult Continuing Education

Pollert A (1988) 'The flexible firm: fixation or fact?' *Work, Employment and Society* 2 (3)

Prais SI (1981) 'Vocational qualifications of the labour force in Britain and Germany' *National Institute Economic Review* 98

Raper P, Ashton D, Feisted A & Storey J (1997) 'Toward the learning organisation?: explaining current trends in training practice in the UK' *International Journal of Training and Development* 1 (1)

Roberts M, McGee N & Payne M (1996) 'Results of the 1995 annual employment survey' *Labour market trends* November Stationery Office, pp487–95

Robinson P (1996) *Rhetoric and reality: Britain's new vocational qualifications* Centre for Economic Performance, London School of Economics

Robinson P (1997) 'The myth of parity of esteem: earnings and qualifications' *Working Paper No 865* Centre for Economic Performance, London School of Economics

Ryan P (1992) (ed) *International comparisons of vocational education and training for intermediate skills* The Falmer Press

Steedman H (1988) 'Vocational training in France and Britain: mechanical and engineering craftsmen' *National Institute Economic Review* 126

Steedman H, Mason G & Wagne K (1991) 'Intermediate skills in the workplace: deployment, standards and supply in Britain, France and Germany' *National Institute Economic Review* 136 2/91

Training Agency (1990) *The training and development of trainers* Training Agency

Unwin L (1994) *Employer involvement in vocational education and training policy: partners or passive recipients?* Unpublished PhD thesis, University of Warwick

Unwin L (1995) *Staying the course: a study of full-time students in South and East Cheshire* South and East Cheshire TEC

Unwin L & Wellington JJ (1995) 'Reconstructing the work-based route: lessons from the modern apprenticeship' *Aspect of Vocational Education* 47 (4)

Vlaeminke M (1990) 'The subordination of technical education in secondary schooling 1870–1914' in P Summerfield & EJ Evans (eds) *Technical education and the state since 1850* Manchester University Press

Watts AG (1983) *Education, unemployment and the future of work* Open University Press

Wellington JJ (1993) *The work-related curriculum* Kogan Page

14. Working to Learn: is New Labour Learning?
A Critique of New Labour's Policies for Work-Related Learning

Karen Evans, Phil Hodkinson, Ewart Keep, Helen Rainbird, Peter Senker, Jim Sutherland & Lorna Unwin

Introduction

In this paper we will argue that, despite some significant improvements to provision for work-related learning, much more remains to be done. We define work-related learning as being 'learning at, for and through the workplace' and which derives its purpose from the context of employment. It should address the needs and interests of a variety of stakeholders including employees, potential employees, employers and government.

Despite a plethora of educational policy documents and pronouncements since the election of a Labour government in 1997, there has been no central policy statement on work-related learning. Rather, approaches to work-related learning appear to be being integrated into broader issues of education and lifelong learning. At first sight, this integration would seem a significant step forward from the climate in which we wrote our first report (see Evans *et al.* 1997). The proposed Learning and Skills Council (LSC) and the local LSCs have a remit to bring together the work-based training, currently managed by Training and Enterprise Councils (TECs), with further and adult education provision. The boundaries between the academic and the vocational are being chipped away at, through, for example: more space for vocational and work-based activity at Key Stage 4; the introduction of common funding and inspection systems; and a new guidance/mentoring service (Connexions). Given the range of proposals in the White Paper *Learning to Succeed* (DfEE, 1999a) and in the report *Bridging the Gap* (Social Exclusion Unit, 1999) we are clearly entering a new era for the provision of learning opportunities in the workplace and elsewhere.

The policy context for this paper is England, and we concentrate mainly on the proposals outlined in the two reports mentioned above. We would suggest, however, that our critique of the impoverished vision for work-related learning and much of what we have to say on issues such as the role of social partnerships, employer investment in training, and work-related learning in general, might apply equally throughout the United Kingdom (UK).

The cornerstone of our proposals in our 1997 report was the notion of 'entitlement'. We argued that young people should be assured that, regardless of where they were in the country and with whatever employer, they would have access to the same standard of vocational education and training. In this improved system, employers would be required to accept and fulfill their responsibilities, rather than simply being told they had the right to play a leading role. In this paper, we want to extend our ideas to adults as well as young people, and to ask whether current policy is up to the task.

Fundamental problems with current approach and vision

Both *Learning to Succeed* and *Bridging the Gap* reflect fundamental problems with the current Government's approach to and positioning of work-related learning. We summarise these as being:

a)   a distorting concentration on full-time education for young people;

b)   a predominantly linear view of progression from learning into work;

c)   an artificial separation of youth and adult provision;

d)   the restriction of some forms of support to those at risk of social exclusion;

e)   an over-emphasis on qualification achievement as a measure of learning success;

f)   a failure to address deep-rooted problems of employment practice;

g)   a narrowly instrumental view of the concept of partnership in lifelong learning;

h)   an over-emphasis on the individual learner;

i)   a failure to address funding and resource issues which act as barriers to access and achievement.

We will address each of these criticisms in turn.

a) *The concentration on full-time education for young people*

Although both *Learning to Succeed* and *Bridging the Gap* are ostensibly focused on improving participation in education, employment and training, prominence is given to the full-time education route. This has been reinforced recently by the Government's aim to get 50% of young people into higher education. Participation of 16–19-year-olds in full-time education has risen over the past 10 years (and stabilised since 1993), whilst, at the same time, numbers entering work-based training have declined.[1] We believe, however, that a revitalised work-based route should be available and, more importantly, could provide much more suitable post-16 provision for many young people who currently drift into staying-on.

There is a flawed assumption in the Government's proposals that a) full-time learning in school or college is superior, and b) that if only we could support, guide and teach young learners properly, they would be well set on the path to unproblematic employment careers. This is encapsulated in Tony Blair's foreword to *Bridging the Gap*: 'The best defence against social exclusion is having a job, and the best way to get a job is to have a good education, with the right training and experience'. (Social Exclusion Unit, 1999: 6)

---

[1] At the end of 1998, 70.5% of 16-year-olds were in full-time education (fte) in England, 9.1% in government-supported training (gst), and 1.4% in employer funded training (eft). The figures at 17 are 58.2% in fte, 10.6% in gst, and 3.3% in eft. (DfEE, 1999b)

Currently, the work-based route is wholly inadequate to meet the needs of both young and adult learners, centred as it is on narrowly-based, task driven NVQs and a voluntaristic approach to employer involvement. Instead, learners need to become members of regulated communities of practice, in which individual and mutual learning involves the acquisition of meaningful theoretical and practical knowledge alongside the practice of skills. It is too early to see who, if anyone, in the new structures, will champion work-related learning at both national and local level.

b) *A linear view of progression*

Closely linked to the educational emphasis, is the explicit assumption that learning happens as a precursor to a successful career. Hence, the Social Exclusion Unit devotes considerable attention to the need to improve educational provision for 16–19-year-olds in order to reduce the numbers of disaffected and disengaged young people. Whilst some of the Unit's proposals are imaginative, the prospects for recovery of those young people whose identities as learners have been most damaged through institutional education are remote. This group includes those who have already been excluded from school and those for whom evidence from the Learning Society programme's research suggests that 'the end of compulsory schooling is very much, at least for the time being, a definite end point to their appetite for education' (Ball *et al.* 1999: 33). The linear view of progression ignores learning at and through work, and crudely simplifies the relationship between institutionalised learning and working life.

c) *The artificial separation of youth and adult provision*

The proposal that the national LSC is to have two separate committees (Youth and Adult) with a separation age cut-off of 19 is problematic. This ignores the blurring of the division between youth and adult caused by increasingly delayed transitions into the labour market, and the fact that the Government's own work-based initiatives (e.g. Modern Apprenticeship, New Deal) follow EU conventions which set the age divide at 25. In their response to *Learning to Succeed,* SKOPE (1999: 4) have suggested that there could be some logic in having the two LSC committees reflect the different dynamics of 'formation' and 'adult, continuing vocational education and training (VET)', but there are two reasons to be cautious: firstly, in the Youth Committee, work-related learning may be marginalised by the more dominant education agenda; and, secondly, the division fails to recognise that in the workplace, and on training schemes, young people and adults have remarkably similar needs and face similar problems.

The White Paper's proposal that the Employment Service should retain responsibility for training the long-term unemployed presents a further fragmentation of policy related to work-related learning.

d) *The restriction of some forms of support to those at risk of social exclusion*

One of the most radical and imaginative proposals in *Learning to Succeed* and *Bridging the Gap* is the new Connexions service (despite the patronising spelling!) to 'create a comprehensive structure for advice and support for all young people beyond 13' (DfEE, 1999a: 51). This will bring together the Careers Service, the Youth Service

121

and other specialist agencies to 'ensure that prompt, co-ordinated action is taken if a young person stops being involved in education or training and risks dropping out' (*ibid*). It would be difficult to argue against greater co-ordination of youth support services, but we are concerned that the focus here is on support as a remedial device rather than on a more holistic approach to guidance pre and post the formal education stage, embracing employment and unemployment, and available whenever necessary.

e) *An over-emphasis on qualification achievement as a measure of learning success*

In the contemporary audit culture, it has become a truism that education has failed unless an appropriate qualification has been achieved. This position is reinforced by the dominance of qualifications in the National Learning Targets and in outcome-related funding. Access to and achievement of appropriate qualifications is clearly extremely important for both young people and adults. Achievement of a qualification usually demonstrates significant learning has occurred, but many people participate in that learning without completing a qualification. This may be out of personal choice or because circumstances dictate that completion of a qualification is not possible for the time being. Using qualifications as the sole measure of learning distorts current policy in ways that may actually increase the damage caused by dropping out, and which marginalise much learning at and through work which is not related to qualification achievement. The former point is illustrated by a paradox of current policy which the White Paper partly acknowledges. The unemployed must always be available for work, but those unemployed people on funded education and training courses must also complete their course. There is a direct conflict here facing many of the very people who are addressed in the Social Exclusion Unit's report.

In our view, two changes are needed. Firstly, the unemployed must be given the right to refuse a poor job, otherwise they are forced in to precisely the sort of downward spiral described in the Unit's report: poor job leads to later unemployment, no skills are learned, and a good job remains out of reach. Secondly, we must accept that, for some, dropping out of a course may be the best option at the time. Such people need to be supported through the 'dropping-out' process and assisted to re-engage with learning at a more suitable later point, rather than being pressurised to struggle on towards gaining a qualification. Learning at, for and through the workplace is a key means of doing this, as exemplified by the *Return to Learn* programme operated by UNISON (see Munro *et al.* 1997).

f) *Failure to address deep-rooted problems of employment practice*

One consequence of the excessive policy focus on educational provision has been the continued failure to tackle England's poor record of employer investment in and support for work-related learning, and the weak state of the training provider infrastructure. The recent report of the Training Standards Council (1999) noted that 50% of training providers for government-supported youth and adult training were so poor as to warrant re-inspection in a year's time. And the network of National Training Organisations (NTOs), whom the White Paper sees as 'pivotal' in 'better engaging employers and defining future skill needs' is made up of, with a few notable exceptions such as the Engineering and Marine Training Authority (EMTA), a motley crew of under-resourced, over-stretched organisations who struggle to carry out their existing duties (DfEE, 1999a: 41).

Employer practices are central not only to learning at and through work, but also to learning for work. Ways need to be found to strengthen work-related communities of practice, including more appropriate regulatory frameworks. For example, in our first report (Evans *et al.* 1997), we advocated legal prohibitions on the full-time employment of under 19-year-olds without proper training provision. Instead, the new Labour government legislated to entitle such employees to time off for training, a much weaker measure than the one we had outlined. As the Social Exclusion Unit report makes clear, there has been very little take-up of this entitlement (which became available in September 1999), a situation which we would argue was entirely predictable. The groups of young people who need legislative support are extremely unlikely to challenge a reluctant employer for access to education and training, let alone take that employer to an industrial tribunal. Furthermore, many such young employees may not, immediately, see the benefits of off-the-job training. This mechanism sends all the wrong signals: paid educational leave is something you have to force out of your employer through legal process in which the inexperienced young worker has to challenge the superior power and resources of the employer. Either their training (on and/or off-the-job) should be made compulsory, as we originally suggested, or they should be given the support and the continued right to secure their entitlement at a later stage, and beyond the cut-off age of 19. Instead, *Bridging the Gap* suggests that the local LSCs be given targets to reduce the number of young people in full-time employment who do not access off-the-job training, without giving the LSCs or the linked Connexions service any teeth.

This deflects attention away from the central question as to how off-the-job provision can best be structured to enhance and supplement informal work-based and near-job training. More generally, it is noticeable throughout government policy that, on the one hand, educational improvement is deemed impossible without tight government control and compulsion, whilst, on the other hand, improvements in adult and work-based provision can only come about through voluntarism. In our view, both approaches are dangerously one-sided.

The principle of paid educational leave is supported by the 1974 International Labour Organisation Convention. This states that, 'Each member (country) shall formulate and apply a policy designed to promote, by methods appropriate to national conditions and practice and by stages as necessary, the granting of paid educational leave for the purposes of (a) training at any level, (b) general, social and civic education, (c) trade union education' (quoted by TUC, 1999: 2). David Chater MP, chair of the All-Party Committee on Adult Education, introduced the *Lifelong Learning (Participation and Entitlement) Bill* in March 1999 to establish an entitlement to paid educational leave. It was a Ten Minute Rule motion, and fell (TUC, 1999: 3). Whereas other countries provide this through a legal entitlement or through collective agreements which have legal force, there is nothing here. The one exception is the flawed statutory entitlement to paid leave for education and training for 16 and 17-year-olds referred to above.

The ongoing fundamental weakness with the Labour government's approach (and that of the Conservative government before it) to work-related learning is the unwillingness to impose any obligation on employers which incurs a cost or promotes workers' rights. The issue of employer contributions to the costs of training their own employees is not addressed. Instead, interventions have focused on labour market supply, in the form of increasing participation rates in further and higher education. Fundamental questions about the nature of employer demand for labour and its deployment in the workplace, which encompass questions of job design and work organisation, are also not addressed. Fundamental questions related to the creation of a work environment which is conducive to learning and to applying new knowledge and skills does not appear in this scenario.

Some progress has, however, been made. The *Employment Relations Act* (1999) has introduced important new rights for trade unions to be consulted on their organisation's workplace training budget and plans. This provides trade unionists with a forum through which they can gain access to information about training and development for the first time. Other social partnership developments have, however, taken a facilitative form rather than establishing rights and entitlements. Both the *University for Industry* and *Individual Learning Accounts* will depend to a large extent on trade unionists' support and endorsement if they are to be accepted by the workforce and used effectively. The DfEE's *Trade Union Learning Fund* has been created to support trade union innovation on learning. A number of the projects are concerned with developing the capacity of trade unionists to provide advice and guidance on learning. Others, potentially, have longer term implications for trade union structures and representational roles. A number of projects are concerned with developing the shop steward's capacity to negotiate on learning issues and UNISON's project on Lifelong Learning Advisers involves a new role of learning advocate within the branch structure. It will be necessary to generalise these 'islands of excellence' to try and show how their features might be replicated across both the public and private sectors.

These measures should be welcomed but they fall short of the strong framework which we believe is required. The first problem is that, although these developments can support workplace learning activity between active trade unions and responsible employers where it is already occurring, it provides no mechanism for extending it to organisations where the employer has no commitment or where trade unions are absent.

The second problem is that the underlying issue of resourcing is not addressed. So long as the resources for investment in training and development are allocated at the employers' discretion, partnership approaches must rely on the employer's self-interest and goodwill. Partnership approaches work best where sources of conflict are removed and the two parties can develop a joint problem-solving approach.

Central to any discussion of work-related learning for both young people and adults is the role of small organisations (under 100 employees). As a society we need the sheer quantity and variety of training places which small organisations have the potential to offer. The practical training and work experience that small firms can provide represents a potentially valuable but neglected national asset. Yet, bearing in mind that small businesses account for half of employment in the UK, and micro businesses (under 10 employees) account for 30% of total employment, there are far fewer training opportunities available in small firms, especially for the young, than there should be.

Left to themselves, small employers are liable to opt for training in job-specific skills rather in broad occupational skills and general education. Most small firms simply do not have access to appropriate resources, training facilities and expertise to offer the broad training that should be provided to give people a sound basis for lifelong learning. If small firms could train more people to meet their own needs for skilled workers, they could reap the benefits of a better trained workforce themselves, producing higher quality products and services, making them more competitive and contributing more to the growth of the national economy. The State should play a role here by promoting partnership between small employers, and partnership between them and education and training providers.

g) *A narrowly instrumental view of partnership in lifelong learning*

The Labour government is to be commended for its policy changes in support of greater partnerships in lifelong learning provision, as embodied in the proposed structures for LSCs at national and local levels. We believe, however, that the government's conception of 'partnership' is still missing an important social dimension.

For example, there is a disconnection between the local Learning and Skills Councils and the wide range of local community stakeholders in lifelong learning, whereas the place of employers appears to have been over-emphasised. In particular, there appears to be only a limited voice at the table for those who might claim to represent learners, and especially disadvantaged learners, be they young people or adults. In our view, more careful thinking is needed about how such voices can be represented and by whom. An increased role for trade unions, local community groups and some providers of guidance support should be considered. Although the new Connexions service could be significant here, there is danger that it will be too tied to meeting government targets on participation and achievement, and so not, necessarily, best placed to operate as advocates for learners in a broader sense.

h) *An over-emphasis on the individual learner*

The major thrusts for adult learning in the government's proposals appear to have a strongly individualist flavour. Much faith, for example, is placed in *Individual Learning Accounts* (ILAs) which require individuals to determine and then invest in their own learning programmes. This is paralleled by the oddly named *University for Industry* which has the appearance of a complex and expensive one-stop shop for training packages, driven by individual customer choices.

This both misunderstands the complexity of decision-making processes, and overlooks the fact that learner decision-making is constrained by unequal power relations and social structures. It equates effective learning with the acquisition of packaged material and experiences. And, importantly, it gives the most vulnerable members of society individual responsibility for solving their own learning problems, rather than addressing the sources of their problems directly. The *Trade Union Learning Fund*, referred to above, is a notable exception here, and, despite the fact that the amount of money available is very small, this initiative might usefully connect to the economic regeneration remit of the Regional Development Agencies (RDAs).

i) *A failure to address funding and resource issues which act as barriers to access and achievement*

The headline-grabbing proposal in *Learning to Succeed* concerns the creation of one funding body, the national LSC, which will replace the Further Education Funding Council (FEFC) and the Training and Enterprise Councils (TECs). This will give the LSC some £5 billion to fund post-16 education and training, though, as yet, not the provision of school sixth forms or higher education. The need to radically transform the archaic and overly complex funding arrangements for the post-16 sector has been advocated for a long time. As SKOPE have pointed out, however, 'while specifying this objective is easy, achieving it is rather less so, and the White Paper is short on details' (SKOPE, 1999: 5). For the purposes of this paper, we will draw attention to some of the funding-related problems that need to be addressed with regard to work-related learning.

In their recent review of the FEFC and TEC funding systems, Felstead & Unwin (1999) identified serious weaknesses with both methodologies. In the case of the TEC system, output-related funding (ORF) has: hindered the provision of high cost occupational areas (e.g. engineering); put pressure on standards and threatened quality of provision; forced some providers to withdraw, thus diminishing the pool; and made it more difficult for trainees who needed extra support (through learning and/or physical disabilities) to enter programmes. The FEFC methodology's emphasis on the amassing of funding units does not reward or provide incentives for colleges to take account of local labour market needs in their curriculum planning. Hence there has been an expansion of courses in nursery nursing and GNVQ courses in leisure and tourism, but too little regard for responding to the needs of local employers. Kennedy (1997: 60) also criticised the FEFC methodology with regard to the 'widening participation' agenda:

> Clever ways have been found of interpreting the funding guidance. Elsewhere, less imagination has been devoted to the task. Analysis of the additional support units claimed by colleges shows wide variation in practice. Funding for widening participation should be a matter of right; not dependent on providers' imagination.

Currently, both the FEFC and TEC funding models are target driven. If we add in the pressures on schools to fill their sixth forms with students who will achieve and, therefore, boost their school's standing in the League Tables, we can see that, at local level, the concept of partnership in the post-16 education and training market is not one based on caring and sharing. The national LSC and the local LSCs will have to work hard to ensure that the new funding arrangements embrace the needs of the very different, and often oppositional, organisations expected to comprise the new Local Learning Partnerships (LLPs)...

As we have previously argued (Evans *et al.* 1997), there are three main beneficiaries of work-related learning, all of whom should bear a part of the costs: employers; the State; and the individual. Employers should expect to fund learning activity that is directly linked to their organisation's central objectives, including the less directly measurable benefits of developing a better skilled and educated workforce. Individuals should expect to pay a contribution towards the cost of their own learning, especially where that learning diverges from the interests of their employer. The State should also pay towards the bill: firstly, because much work-related learning directly contributes to central policy objectives such as social inclusion and citizenship; and secondly, because the State has a responsibility to support those members of society who lack the resources to improve their employability skills.

Conclusion

Building on our earlier proposals (see Evans *et al.* 1997), we argue that there is still an overwhelming need to promote and develop high quality work-related learning opportunities for both young people and adults. The ideas presented here form the first stage in the development of our second report in which we will outline our ideas regarding entitlement to high quality work-related learning and the ways in which such learning should be enhanced.

References

Ball SJ, Macrae S & Maguire M (1999) 'Young lives at risk in the "futures" market: some policy concerns from ongoing research' in F Coffield (ed) *Speaking truth to power* The Policy Press

DfEE (1999a) *Learning to succeed: a new framework for post-16 learning* The Stationery Office

DfEE (1999b) 'Participation in education and training by 16–18 year olds in England, 1988–1998' *Statistical First Release SFR13/1999* DfEE

Evans K, Hodkinson P, Keep E, Maguire M, Raffe D, Rainbird H, Senker P & Unwin L (1997) 'Working to learn, a work-based route for young people' *Issues in People Management No.18* Institute for Personnel and Development

Felstead A & Unwin L (1999) *Funding systems and their impact on skills* Skills Task Force Research Paper 11 DfEE

Kennedy H (1997) *Learning works: widening participation in further education* FEFC

Munro A, Rainbird H & Holly L (1997) *Partners in workplace learning* Unison

SKOPE (1999) *Response to the DfEE's consultations on the White Paper: Learning to Succeed* ESRC Centre for Skills, Knowledge & Organisational Performance

Social Exclusion Unit (1999) *Bridging the gap: new opportunities for 16–18 year olds not in education, employment or training* The Stationery Office

TUC (1999) *Paid educational leave* Trades Union Congress

15.   New Deal and the Colleges

Ken Marsh

Introduction[1]

This paper is an evaluative summary of research undertaken by a self-selected team within the London Region Post-16 Network, who over a period of nine months conducted an investigation into how a central plank in the UK Government's policy to combat social exclusion, namely the New Deal, was operating within selected FE colleges in London and the South East.

The New Deal applies at present to unemployed people of all ages up to the age of 50 (a 50+ New Deal is about to be introduced), although the research concentrated on the scheme as it operates for the 18–24 age group.

After six months of unemployment a young person is brought into the scheme and passes through various stages. The first stage is 'Gateway' where the client is allocated a New Deal Personal Adviser (NDPA), who will counsel, assess, advise and support him/her over a period of up to six months (longer for the over 25s). If that person within that time has not found work then he/she is counselled into one of four options over a six to twelve month period:

1) subsidised employment, with at least one day's education and training per week (employers are offered £75 a week per trainee plus a £750 contribution towards training costs);

2) a job with the Government environment task force which includes day release education and training on an accredited training scheme;

3) a job with a voluntary sector employer, again with day release training towards an approved qualification;

4) up to 12 months' full-time education and training (FTET) in a college or other training provider, leading to a Level 2 NVQ or equivalent qualification.

This last is proving to be the most popular option and it is on this that our research was focused.

The philosophy behind the New Deal

The central purpose is to lead the long-term unemployed from benefit dependence into work. The policy itself derives from the observation that, compared to the USA, long-term unemployment in Europe (defined as those out of work for over one year) is strikingly high. Professor Layard, of the London School of Economics, believes the

---

[1] This is a summary of a research paper presented to a conference sponsored by the London Region Post-16 Network at the University of London Institute of Education on 20 June, 2000.

reason for this lies in an over-generous unemployment benefits system operating in many EU countries which acts as a disincentive to the long-term unemployed to enhance their skills and find work.

In the USA many benefits stop after one year and it is at this point one sees a dramatic difference between the EU and USA in the numbers of long-term unemployed. Layard (1999a) does not argue for a USA-type benefits system, which he feels is too harsh and contributes to 2% of the male population ending up in jail. He proposes taking benefits money and using it to generate jobs or support training. The training support is given through some form of individual activity which will promote an individual's employability.

This idea links in with New Labour's 'third way' philosophy, namely that the state will assist an individual back into employment only if that individual acts responsibly in seeking to improve his/her employability. It recognises that long-term unemployment is a social waste and that the longer a person is unemployed the less employers are interested in employing him/her. The New Deal seeks to break the cycle of long-term unemployment through training the individual and reintroducing him/her into the labour market. It does this by changing the role of the Employment Service from a jobs matching vacancies role to a role where it is active in counselling and placing people into subsidised jobs or training. It is at this point that two concepts in the philosophy behind the New Deal operate. The first is the idea of 'Stock and Flow', the second is the 'Lump of Labour Fallacy'.

Stock and flow

Layard asserts that at this point in time there are many long-term unemployed who have become accustomed to a generous benefits culture and are neither motivated nor sufficiently skilled to find work or be offered employment. They are already settled into a dependency culture. This group, Layard argues, constitutes the existing 'stock' and will be very difficult to motivate into the work ethic or to retrain. It appears that many in this group, under threat of loss of benefits, are choosing the college training option of the New Deal. However, once this existing stock has been dealt with, Layard asserts, then we shall have a flow of people who will (because of the New Deal) not be allowed to drift into a dependency culture and as such there will be less cultural dependency baggage to cause problems in the future.

The lump of labour fallacy

One criticism of the New Deal is made by those economists who assert that if the government subsidises people into jobs this interferes with the jobs market by providing cheap labour. Layard believes that this idea is false as it is based on the 'fallacy' that the number of jobs in the economy is static. Again he looks to the example of the last five years in the USA (1995–2000), where the labour force increased by 25%, and it was noted that the number of jobs over the same period went up also by 25%. In his view the number of jobs in an economy is determined by the effective supply of labour as seen by employers. This is the essential idea behind the New Deal in its attempt to upskill the long-term unemployed. The trouble, as Layard states, is that few countries believe it. As a result, those countries in the EU which operate on a static employment policy will be saddled with a large underclass of long-term unemployed already well entrenched into a dependency culture. A controversial position is taken by Layard when he asserts that even in unemployment problem areas there is a thriving economy and labour market often less than an hour's travel away. Those in a dependency culture need to be persuaded to travel, he maintains, if they are to climb out of their dependency – shades of 'Get on yer bike' here, one may fancy. It is not surprising that attitudes are difficult to change. Skewing the benefits system to change attitudes is at the heart of the New Deal.

Method of investigation

The study and evaluation were carried out over a 6-month period from September 1999 to March 2000. Research methods used were a combination of questionnaires sent out to 20 colleges within London and the South East, followed through with telephone reminders and later in-depth interviews with a selection of college New Deal co-ordinators. All 20 colleges returned their questionnaires. The interviews were structured around key issues and concerns arising out of an analysis of the questionnaire returns.

I will list the main findings and try to outline what might be an ideal New Deal experience for those clients choosing the college education and training option. Anyone involved with a college New Deal scheme may be surprised at the different responses we received. It would be true to say that a great variety of individual schemes have been negotiated between colleges and representatives of the Employment Service. Nothing, it might almost be said, is non-negotiable.

General findings

1. Poor basic skills and attitudinal and motivational problems

It was found that non-completion/drop out rates were high, with many 'New Dealers' severely lacking in both basic and attitudinal skills. One college located in an area with a high concentration of people from minority ethnic groups found severe ESOL difficulties in the clients referred to them and responded by setting up Saturday ESOL classes in an attempt to take them up to an employable standard.

In one or two colleges some tutors or heads of departments had developed hostile attitudes to New Deal clients, owing to their persistent lateness, absences, or failure to turn up for interviews. This finding coincides with a piece of research conducted by Youthaid which noted that in the present buoyant economy many New Deal clients are finding work during the Gateway period, leaving the more challenging people for the college education and training option (Slater, 2000). It seems that this issue of attitudinal and basic skills deficit is a real challenge for the colleges.

2. The tension between the longer term focus on employability and the short term focus on meeting job targets

Considerable frustration was experienced by New Deal co-ordinators over the Employment Service limits on a) time to rectify basic deficit skills, and b) progression to higher grade programmes. One year was often felt to be too short to complete a vocational course, say in media studies, or to acquire appropriate GCSEs.

In some cases this could cause considerable frustration on the part of both the New Dealers and the teaching staff.

It was noted in our investigations that there was a considerable amount of 'rule bending' by New Deal co-ordinators to get round these limitations to access and progression and to attempt to build more flexibility into the system. Indeed we found some ingenious 'accommodations' and 'understandings' between local Employment Service personal advisers and college New Deal co-ordinators, which had allowed individuals to progress through to level three and access programmes. Given that the New Deal is aimed at preparation for employment rather than progression into higher education, this was a most interesting finding.

3. Mismatch between roll-on-roll-off New Deal delivery pattern and college organisational structures – new wine in old bottles?

It was found across the colleges that much depended on the individual efforts and commitment of the New Deal co-ordinators in attempting to fit an over-conceived flexibility and individually-tailored programme of 30 hours a week throughout a fifty-week year into a college framework operating over a shorter academic year, combined with a less flexible curriculum delivery pattern. This was not true in all the colleges investigated, nor across all departments within a college.

This finding is reinforced by Keith Sherlock, Chief Inspector of the Training Standards Council (Slater, 2000), who reported that there was too much 'shoe-horning' of New Dealers into existing programmes. The issue of infilling New Deal clients into existing course programmes on the basis of cost effectiveness also related to a finding that in some colleges New Deal students were barred from taking more materials-costly courses such as photography or art on the grounds that it would be too expensive for the college and that in any case the one year allowed would be too short a time to complete the study programme. Infilling in the pursuit of cost-effectiveness often resulted in students being placed on programmes for which they were unsuitable or uninterested and was one reason cited by course co-ordinators for non-completion or drop out.

4. High drop out rates

Drop out rates were high, averaging around 55%, though there were some noted successes (81% retention in one college) with a small number of students moving into level 3 and in one or two cases onto HND level 4 programmes, though there was some doubt as to whether such progression was totally within the spirit of New Deal.

Reasons cited by New Deal co-ordinators for drop out were:

- *Attitudinal:* Some students believed the college option would be a soft option but then found that they often lacked the basic skills to sustain them through a course programme.
- *Motivational:* Some are placed on the wrong programme of study.
- *Stigmatising:* Because New Dealers had to sign on and off, and did not share the half-term and holiday breaks of FEFC-funded students, many felt labelled and discriminated against. This affected their often already low self esteem.

- *Staff attitude:* In a few cases, tutors themselves were hostile or unwelcoming to New Deal students being 'dropped' into the middle of an existing programme.
- *Programme content and planning:* Some found the programmes irrelevant or too theoretical, with too little work placement or training provision.

5. Colleges' organisational and financial problems

It was not surprising to find that college management information structures were geared towards FEFC-funded students and not designed to cope with New Deal roll-on-roll-off programmes. Colleges, by and large, were losing financially by taking on New Deal trainees (one college claimed that the per capita administrative costs came to £350 compared with £150 for an FEFC-funded student). Some colleges responded by limiting course option choices to areas which needed least resourcing, so that students wishing to take up photography for example would find this option closed because of financial constraints by the college. Colleges themselves responded differently to taking on New Deal.

Those colleges in more affluent areas with aspirations of taking on more HE work were, unsurprisingly, unenthusiastic or poorly prepared for New Deal clients who themselves were few in number. Those colleges in high unemployment areas had already responded more positively and constructively in meeting the needs of New Deal clients and it is to these colleges that we must turn if we wish to distil what might be best practice in delivering the college option more successfully.

6. Staff training and induction

Our research found considerable variation between colleges with regard to in-service preparation and training for staff, many of whom would be involved in catering for New Deal students. For those colleges with little or no in-service training much of the burden fell on the New Deal co-ordinators and there was considerable cynicism from staff as to whether the programme would work. There were numerous complaints also about the amount of clerical work which New Deal co-ordinators had to work through to satisfy Employment Service regulations.

Best practice distilled

Our research was conducted in a positive spirit and in the belief that New Deal can make a difference. A successful structure for the delivery of the New Deal college option might look something like this:

1. A close partnership between the NDPAs and New Deal co-ordinators

In some colleges this was achieved by placing Gateway provision, in consultation with personal advisers, in the college. This arrangement also helps to break down concepts in the minds of New Dealers that the New Deal Personal Adviser is part of the job centre establishment.

2. More flexibility in progression and access and more time to complete programmes

A question arises as to whether the New Deal is excessively employment-focused. Should New Dealers have formal access to academic courses as well as vocational ones?

3. Better guidance and support systems

Some colleges and NDPAs brought in private specialist help for career guidance, in the belief that correct diagnosis of vocational and career needs was of prime importance in preventing drop-out. The question arises here as to whether NDPAs have too much to do and are sufficiently skilled or trained to do it. Some colleges had linked into referral support agencies such as those for drug or alcohol dependence.

4. Tighter support structure

The problems associated with infilling, where often New Dealers feel scattered and unsupported, need to be overcome. One college has set up a New Deal base in one of its Learning Resource Centres, where New Dealers can meet and discuss issues with a New Deal support staff team of three, and where they can access job search and get further help with key skills on a drop-in-at-any-time approach and where all New Dealers have their individually-tailored action plans worked out for them. Retention rates for New Dealers at this college are already at 81% and rising. It may be noted that this college attempts to place New Deal clients at the start of each unit on a particular programme, and that it provides subsidised hot meals for around £1.50.

5. Staffing

Successful New Deal structures are also associated with kindly, supportive and welcoming staff who have received induction and training around New Deal issues and have a commitment to the values behind inclusive learning.

6. Simplified administrative procedures and funding to support individualised programmes according to need

There were many complaints by New Deal co-ordinators over the amount of time-consuming checking and 'red tape'. In addition, financially-strapped colleges need to be supported in their efforts to deliver individually-tailored programmes based on client need rather than efficiency and cost-effectiveness.

Conclusion

The successes of New Deal students are beginning to show in those colleges which have a political and organisational commitment to it. Despite problems with drop-out and rigid college structures, co-ordinators reported individual success stories of how some clients had reported gaining in confidence and making new friends as new skills were realised. In the words of one co-ordinator: 'Yes there are some people who are unemployable; however there are a good many individual success stories. The idea of New Deal is sound – it can and does change lives!'

References

Layard R (1999a) *Tackling inequality* Macmillan

Layard R (1999b) *The thinking behind New Deal* Open Lecture Institute of Education post-16 centre, March 16th

Slater J (2000) 'Hardest nut yet to be cracked' *Times Education Supplement* March 31st

Part Five – Professionalism, Policies and Values

The final contributions to this Reader bring together our three principal themes: the nature of the professional commitment of teachers and trainers in the post-16 sector, the formation and implementation of the policies which control their activities, and the framework of values which supports (and perhaps subverts) the levels of professional involvement in the work of our PCET institutions.

Keith Randle and Norman Brady provide a case study of how the re-organisation of a college management structure after incorporation produced a new type of management style, with a different value system, which challenged the culture of the lecturers and called into question their professionalism and autonomy.

Differences between the perceptions of senior managers and teaching staff is also evident in the last extract, from a joint churches working party report on values in the FE curriculum. We should not be surprised that organised religious groups wish to contribute to the debate about institutional and personal values, and the framework which is presented here brings this volume to a thoughtful close.

We have surveyed many aspects of professionalism: issues concerned with the training, the continuing development of practice through reflection, and the relationship between professional expertise, the management of institutions and the implementation of policy.

However difficult it may be to say precisely what we mean by the term 'professional', we might end by agreeing with Noble & Pym (1970) that the principal defining characteristic of professionals is their 'avowal of a code of practice which commits [them] to the independent exercise of [their] own trained judgement'. We need to ensure that no policies and no institutions of education and training undermine those values or threaten that professional judgement.

Reference

Noble T & Pym B (1970) 'Collegial authority and the receding locus of power' *British Journal of Sociology* 21, pp431–445

16. Managerialism and Professionalism in the 'Cinderella Service'

Keith Randle & Norman Brady

Introduction[1]

Whilst there has been considerable academic interest in the impact of recent, government-imposed changes in the primary and secondary sectors of state education in the UK, the UK further education (FE) sector has been largely ignored. There has been virtually no independent work published based on research in the area (though see Elliott, 1996), but it has been noted in the press that whilst the sector appears all but invisible:

> It costs the taxpayer more than £2.5 billion a year; provides work for more than *100,000* people and has two and a half million clients. The workers are revolting, the customers are complaining, the police are investigating and *100* of its chief executives have suffered votes of no confidence. It is a big business in big trouble, but no-one seems to care.
>
> Last week it was rocked by strikes and hardly anyone noticed. We are talking about further education – the Cinderella service that caters for more of the over *16* population than all the schools and universities put together.
>
> (*The Guardian*, 12 March 1995: 11)

The FE sector has traditionally provided the bulk of technical education and vocational preparation within the UK system, and it has been suggested that the academic value system has accorded this type of education little attention and low priority (McGinty & Fish, 1993). This may go some way towards accounting for the 'invisibility' of the sector'. Now, however, certain government objectives are seen as achievable through the current strategy in Further Education.

By boosting student numbers in FE the government can deflect opposition criticism of the poor UK record in post-16 education compared to other European states. Indeed, there are those who go so far as to see, in increased student numbers, a newly-found government commitment to FE as the source of a future highly-skilled and flexible workforce, the key to effective industrial and commercial competition (McGinty & Fish, 1993).

Themes of common interest can be identified running through all sectors of UK state education and this paper will identify issues in FE common to much of the public sector as a whole. However, it is also important to recognise that change in the public sector has not been even in pace, depth nor in the response of employees and that caution must be exercised in making generalisations (Kirkpatrick *et al.* 1996).

The purpose of the paper is to situate recent changes in the structure, funding and management of the FE sector within debates around what has been called the 'New Public Service Management' (Walsh, 1995), the 'New Public Management' Kirkpatrick *et al.* 1996), or simply the 'New Managerialism' (Pollitt, 1990; Farnham & Horton, 1993; Flynn, 1993).

The paper arises from case study research carried out at Cityshire College[2] and involved a programme of interviews with senior management and a staff attitude questionnaire. During the period September to December 1994, semi-structured interviews were conducted with a cross-section of College managers. An attitude survey of lecturers was conducted during the spring of 1995. Questionnaires were distributed to 360 lecturers and 172 responses were received.

The background to change

In 1988 the Education Reform Act began the process of removing further education from the control of the Local Education Authorities (LEAs) and major responsibilities for finance, management and college development were delegated to Governing Bodies (McGinty & Fish, 1993). Cityshire College was formed from a merger of four separate Further Education colleges in 1991 and by 1993, had approximately 42,000 enrolments, the equivalent of 7000 full-time students. The College staff numbered about 2000 in total, including 400 full-time lecturers and for 1993/4 Cityshire had a budget income of over £31 million. The merger of former specialist colleges offering regional provision with local colleges produced a new institution encompassing a relatively wide spread of vocational and non-vocational education. Cityshire contains a mixture of non-advanced further education (NAFE) and advanced further education (AFE) provision.

The second Act to have a major effect on the management of colleges was the 1992 Further and Higher Education Act which provided for the setting up of non-elected Boards to manage incorporated colleges. Whilst incorporation has meant increased autonomy for Cityshire from the Local Education Authority, since 1993 the responsibility for the availability and quality of further education has rested with the Further Education Funding Council for England (FEFCE) which provides approximately 60% of Cityshire's income. In reality, therefore, further education is largely controlled by central government through this agency. Funding for educational provision is dependent on the college fulfilling certain performance targets. Failure to retain students or failure of students to complete courses successfully will result in 'claw back' of funds. In addition to these performance criteria, the FEFCE stipulate that Cityshire must satisfy certain quality assurance measures such as the regular testing of college services through student surveys and a formal monitoring of course provision. The FEFCE, therefore, is a crucial agency in influencing the management of the college at both the strategic and operational levels, and it could be argued that it has driven the scale, shape and pace of change in the FE system in England since incorporation.

Incorporation and independence: the experience at Cityshire

In the initial post-incorporation period, senior management at Cityshire at first appeared to take action with little regard as to how it might be perceived by college staff. For example, in 1992 a number of planning teams were set up at the college, under the guidance of a hired consultant, to produce reports on the possible organisation of college functions such as marketing, internal communication, and staff training and development. However, little feedback on how these recommendations were received by senior management was given, either to the team members or to other members of the lecturing staff. A further example was that of the Senior Management Team (SMT) ordering lease cars for senior managers and the conduct of a high profile official post-incorporation College launch against a background of deep staff anxiety, and uncertainty about the future, particularly the college's financial future. For the academic staff these initiatives represented potent symbols of a 'new order' which did not sit well with ominous statements from the Principal about the seriousness of the budget position. The perception of the authors was one of increasing cynicism amongst lecturers about the style of management being adopted in the college.

Interviews with representatives of senior management suggested that central to their thinking was the belief that lecturers had simply not grasped the political and economic realities of the situation in which the college found itself. The management's position was that the college must expand its provision over the coming years in order to receive adequate funding and therefore remain financially viable. There appeared to be an unstated assumption that the conditions of service of academic staff (the 'silver book' agreement) were over-generous and untenable. Senior management, however, acknowledged that the changes had not been communicated effectively to the staff and that internal communications were generally weak within the college.

Throughout the 1992–94 period, the Principal appeared to have gradually recognised the need to convince the academic staff of the need for change, particularly as industrial relations deteriorated. The Principal took to visiting the constituent schools within the college to meet academic staff and explain impending changes. A college bulletin was produced more regularly. College-wide rituals were instituted such as regular end of term social events attended by senior managers. A staff appraisal system was established which in its embryonic state represented a 'soft' developmental approach (Legge, 1989) aimed at identifying training needs associated with the achievement of agreed objectives and was not linked to promotion or reward.

The Senior Management Team's analysis of the organisational dysfunction experienced within the college was based largely on the assumption that it was the inevitable consequence of wide-ranging and deep organisational change implemented at too fast a pace. Operational management failures were, therefore, a natural result of teething problems. The SMT also acknowledged that a gap in management expertise existed as former academics, now occupying management positions, grappled with problems which required a range of new management skills.

A senior manager commented:

... what we have in FE is a set of people who were never trained as managers, who are running scared at the moment because of the way I am making them accountable for their actions, for the way in which I have them on performance

139

pay and very, very tight accountabilities. They feel vulnerable, they feel frightened...

In an effort to overcome these problems the SMT instituted training programmes for managers, aimed mainly at improving systems management. In some respects the 'too deep, too fast' analysis is correct, and helps account for operational dysfunction. However, it pays little attention to the fundamental causes of lecturer resistance.

We later argue that the cause of this dysfunction is concerned with the impact upon professional autonomy of the new management style practised at Cityshire following incorporation. First, however, we continue with an account of what we have earlier referred to as 'the new managerialism'.

The new managerialism

The new managerialism can be characterised as a style of management which emerged in the UK in the early 1980s and gradually spread throughout the Public Sector. It began with the Civil Service in the wake of the Rayner Scrutinies and the Financial Management Initiative (Metcalf & Richards, 1987) and has since been established in local authorities, the BBC, the NHS and the Education sector.

Pollitt (1990) argues that new managerialism can be understood as a generic package of management techniques which include:

- strict financial management and devolved budgetary controls
- the efficient use of resources and the emphasis on productivity
- the extensive use of quantitative performance indicators
- the development of consumerism and the discipline of the market
- the manifestation of consumer charters as mechanisms for accountability
- the creation of a disciplined, flexible workforce, using flexible/individualised contracts, staff appraisal systems and performance related pay
- the assertion of managerial control and the managers' right to manage.

Underpinning the new managerialism are the assumptions first that 'good management' will deliver the three 'Es' of economy, efficiency and effectiveness in public services and therefore can ensure value for taxpayers' money and eliminate waste (Metcalf & Richards, 1987). Secondly, that 'good management' did not exist in the public sector prior to 1979.

John Major, as Chief Secretary to the Treasury, speaking to the Audit Commission in 1989, said of the public sector prior to the election of the Conservative government:

The effects of this system were pernicious. It made the public sector a preferential creditor on the economy as a whole ... it undermined the value for money and deprived the public sector and its management of the main and most natural incentive to improve its efficiency and control its costs.

(Major, 1989: 3)

'Good management' was to be found in the private sector, where management was superior to the tradition of 'administration' in the public sector (Kirkpatrick & Martinez Lucio, 1995). Its essence could be distilled as a generic package of skills and techniques which could then be applied as a template for public sector institutions. Privatisation and the marketisation of public sector institutions therefore would improve the three 'Es'.

This brief analysis of new managerialism and its political and ideological origins is relevant to the situation at Cityshire college in a number of respects. It partly explains the context in which the organisational changes have come about and particularly the motives behind FEFCE's directives to the management of Colleges. More specifically, it locates the management style adopted by SMT at Cityshire in the context of a public sector policy designed simultaneously to expand further education and to shift the burden of funding down to the college itself, through pressure to develop its own plans for income generation.

This also helps to explain why the conflict with lecturers at Cityshire is, in fact, being replicated in a variety of forms in management/professional relationships throughout the public sector (Gunn, 1988; Pollitt, 1990; Stewart & Walsh, 1992; Hoggett, 1994).

If efficiency gains are to be achieved in further education then it is to the new breed of academic managers that the responsibility for their delivery falls. In order to achieve such gains, we argue, control over the conception and design of academic work is increasingly being taken away, by management, from practitioners responsible for its delivery in the classroom, and placed in the hands of specialist managers or external agencies. This reflects the process of deskilling that Braverman (1975) asserts craft labour has undergone during the twentieth century.

The process has also been identified as taking place in higher education (Miller, 1991), with some authors (Parker & Jary, 1995) going so far as to adopt a 'neo-Fordist' label to describe what they argue represents a move away from 'elite specialisation with strong professional control', towards a Fordist mass production arrangement which, borrowing from Ritzer (1993), they term the 'McUniversity'. In the sections which follow we explore the conflict a comparable process has prompted at Cityshire.

Conflicting paradigms

The changes which were implemented at Cityshire met lecturer resistance in the form of both covert and overt action. An example of covert action was the common practice, by lecturers, of non-cooperation with official surveys and a regular failure to return questionnaires. In terms of overt resistance, national negotiations over new flexible contracts between the largest of the lecturers' unions, the National Association of Teachers in Further and Higher Education (NATFHE) and the national employers' organisation, the College Employers' Forum (CEF)[3], began in November 1993 and have since remained in impasse. Local negotiations between the Principal and the Cityshire branch of NATFHE also reached impasse, and between December 1994 and August 1995 the two sides were in official dispute.

We have characterised the clash in values that we identify at Cityshire as one between 'managerialism' and 'professionalism'. Elliott (1996: 8) uses a similar dichotomy to describe the 'pervasive market ideology, implemented by senior managers who seemed to embrace a managerialist culture' in his case study of an FE college, which contrasted with 'the competing democratic ideology underpinned by a commitment to a student-centred pedagogic culture' held by lecturers. In Table 1 we summarise what we regard as the main areas for potential conflict between managers and FE professionals.

Professional paradigm	Managerialist paradigm
Goals and values • primacy of student learning and the teaching process • loyalty to students and colleagues • concern for academic standards	• primacy of student through-put and income generation • loyalty to the organisation • concern to achieve an acceptable balance between efficiency and effectiveness
Key assumptions • lecturers as funds of expertise • resources deployed on the basis of educational need • quality of provision assessed on the basis of input	• lecturers as flexible facilitators and assessors • resources deployed on the basis of market-demand and value for taxpayers' money • quality assessed on the basis of output/outcomes
Management ethos • collegiality/'community of practice' • professional autonomy/the trust principle/accountability to peers/tacit knowledge • pluralism	• control by managers and the market • management by performance indicators and surveillance • unitarism

Table 1 Conflicting paradigms

However, 'professionals' and 'the professions' are terms which have generated a lengthy and largely unresolved debate in the sociological literature; indeed, sociological analysis of the professions has been described as 'in turmoil' (Rueschemeyer, 1983: 38). However, it is important to situate our choice of the term within a literature which has sought to contain two apparently conflicting perspectives; 'on the one hand, professions are seen as uniquely ethical occupations; on the other as powerful groups who have masked their pursuit of self-interest behind essentially spurious ethical codes' (Crompton, 1990: 147).

In the case of further education lecturers we do not consider the second of these perspectives to be helpful. It would require a considerable stretch of the imagination to characterise lecturers as a 'powerful group' in the way that perhaps those occupations based upon medicine, accountancy or the law may be characterised. There is no powerful representative professional association and no ability to ensure market closure and the group has relatively little opportunity to limit entry into the profession. However, that perspective which emphasises the 'uniquely ethical occupations' displaying the 'institutionalised altruism' necessary when expert labour is harnessed for the benefit of a client (Crompton, 1990), whilst not necessarily peculiar to professional occupations, may be of more value in situating college lecturers. Burrage & Torstendahl (1990) identify a number of key features of post-war public service 'professional' work which could be applied to pre-incorporation further education and which include: the presence of expert, tacit knowledge and skills; professional autonomy over work in terms of decision-making and implementation; work perceived as socially useful and implicitly anti-commercial; the relationship with the client being one of loyalty whilst the locus of power rests with the professional; the attainment of high standards in the execution of work-related tasks; and the organisation of the work on the basis of collegiality.

This can be characterised as a 'public service ethic' where the prime concern is to provide 'quality educational opportunities for students', and where the emphasis on business systems and efficiency is alien to many (Dearing, 1994: 3). That there are contrasting sets of values is underlined by the fact that 84.6% of respondents to the attitude survey believed that the college management did not share the same educational values as the lecturers.

Under the pre-incorporation public service model the professional's position and relative autonomy were underwritten by a well-established set of external institutional relationships with, for example, examination boards and professional bodies, which ensured considerable control over course content and teaching methods. Despite the intervention in issues of pay and funding by central and local government, and the regular industrial disputes which resulted, the lecturers and the colleges as a whole nevertheless operated in a climate of relative stability. However, government education policy over the last decade, and in particular over the last two years, has radically undermined the lecturers' sense of security in a number of different ways.

Most significant has been the radical intervention in the management of FE colleges by the FEFCs. In the case of Cityshire it is the dynamic created by the FEFC's funding strategy which has done most to disempower the lecturers at college level. The erstwhile administrative manager, from Head of Department upward, has been replaced by a new type of manager operating on a different agenda. Traditionally, there was the perception that staff and managers aspired to a common set of educational values, encompassing the notion of a degree of professional expertise and some discretion in the design, delivery and assessment of provision. This commonality rested on the fact that funding was not dependent on satisfying detailed, externally imposed, requirements concerning the size and nature of the student body. However, it is worth noting that Gorringe (Gorringe & Togood, 1994) takes a less positive view of pre-incorporation funding mechanisms, arguing that the shift from an 'allocation' to an 'earning' model represents a shift 'from an unequal struggle with a capricious allocator of funds, to the need to attract, retain and delight paying customers, whether they be a quango, a private company or an individual citizen' (Gorringe & Togood, 1994: 186).

The new managers are primarily concerned with resource management, particularly financial resources (Warner & Crosthwaite, 1995). Many lecturers at Cityshire saw management as being obsessed with budgets and business plans as against their own concerns for the client. However, one Cityshire senior manager justified this, with an argument that new managerialism offers potential productivity gains which will ultimately benefit the client:

> *The thing that the old public sector approach did was to spend large volumes of money quite wastefully, and what we can do with a better focused use of resources is actually get more people involved in education.*

'Quality' in further education

The drive to increase student numbers was perceived by lecturers in this study to have caused a serious dilution in the quality of educational provision in some areas of the college. There was concern expressed by lecturers that students were being recruited for courses for which they were not academically equipped. The lecturers also expressed concern that many students were being retained on courses regardless of their performance and, in some cases, despite near certainty of failure. This would represent a short-term strategy as, under the funding methodology, the college would be subject to financial penalties where there was evidence of student failure, or a lack of 'impartial guidance'. However, 61.8% of lecturers in the attitude survey felt that public examination standards had declined between 1992 and 1994. Reluctance by the Heads of Schools to lose students could, however, be attributed to the fact that the student (or 'unit of activity') was worth approximately £2000. A proportion of this money, related to length of stay in the college, would be 'clawed back' if the student dropped out (Nash, 1994). This process has now been divided into a bi-annual exercise with funding applied in three post-review tranches.

The question of quality provides a good illustration of the clash between managerial and professional values. Lecturers felt that their professional judgement and control over the educational process was being displaced by that of managers, and that the quality of the provision, as they understood it, was being undermined as a result. Eighty per cent of respondents to the attitude survey thought that organisational changes had not improved the quality of service to students, and 95% of respondents thought that the changes as a whole had not enhanced student learning. On the other hand, a senior manager described how 'quality' could be seen in the opportunities the changes had given to young people previously excluded from the system:

> *One aspect of the quality (of education) and the measurement of the quality of the institution is how much of the potential student population is being served... Putting it very fundamentally you can have fewer students and give them a Rolls Royce experience or you can have millions of students, each of them getting a Mini, and provided the Mini works, then that is better quality*

144

in terms of the fact that you are empowering, enabling and providing for many more people than you would otherwise have done.

'Quality', viewed from this perspective, does not conform with the commonly held assumption of an association with goods or services of a superior or exceptionally high standard. However, it does accord closely with the definitions provided by the experts and quality gurus who describe quality as 'conformance to requirements'. Thus, however 'inferior' a product may be in absolute terms, as long as it consistently meets the standards that beat the competition within its market niche, a good or service can be regarded as having quality (Wilkinson & Willmott, 1995). Lecturers at Cityshire, however, perceived this as a *post hoc* rationalisation of the central government policy of stimulating rapid expansion in the further education system, without commensurate levels of investment.

Wilkinson & Willmott (1995: 3) go on to argue that the logic of 'conformance to requirements' can also be applied to the organisation of work and that quality, in this case, means 'the development of "uniform and dependable" work practices that are congruent with delivering products at low cost with a quality suited to the market'. In order to develop such work practices within further education, we argue, it has been necessary to further reduce professional control and introduce a form of 'Neo-Taylorism'. It is to this that we now turn.

The decline of professional control

The government-inspired movement to shift to competence-based assessment of vocational courses validated by the National Council for Vocational Qualifications has begun to reposition the lecturer as an assessor, concerned with measuring student performance, rather than a teacher, facilitating student learning. The content and assessment of these courses are so highly prescribed that lecturers feel a loss of control over the teaching process. Hence, respondents to the questionnaire typically included comments to the effect that the degree of assessment required by GNVQ forced lecturers to divert their efforts away from the teaching process. Assessment has thus become an onerous and time consuming activity. Sixty-four per cent of attitude survey respondents felt that new assessment methods had reduced their level of job satisfaction as a result.

Concerns about control over course content and modes of delivery are reflected in feelings about the implications of 'flexible-learning'. What concerned a number of lecturers was the particular vision of flexi-learning outlined by SMT at Cityshire, and which is still in its embryonic stages. The picture painted by the Principal was one of students spending a sizeable proportion of their time in independent study using banks of pre-packaged materials and computer technology in a model of 'independent learning' based on the American Community School. The Principal is attracted by the potential productivity gains of this learning mode where lecturer-student contact hours could be cut by the application of multi-media technology which employs such techniques as video-conferencing. Lecturers could therefore be asked to teach more, and shorter, classes, and pressure on teaching accommodation would be reduced as distance learning increased. Lecturer resistance to information technology is explained by senior managers as being based on a stubborn retention of outmoded attitudes to teaching:

> *The problem we have got is the lack of acceptance on the part of the average teacher that there is a different or better way of doing it, and part of the problem is the very human problem of not wanting to believe that technology can actually do a big chunk of their work better than they can.*

(Senior Manager)

For lecturers, the implications of this are enormous, with the emphasis in the learning process shifting from classroom interaction to the teaching materials themselves. There has been an increasing reliance on pre-packaged materials bought in by the College and which has led to a further decline in lecturer control over the content and use of teaching materials. However, at Cityshire, the Principal's belief that teaching is to a large extent the imparting of factual knowledge which can be effectively achieved through multi-media packages is disputed by the staff. While this theme was not addressed by the questionnaire and cannot be quantified, it is the perception of the authors, based on informal discussions with staff, that transference of factual knowledge is seen, by the latter, as minor compared to the teaching of skills required, for example, in the analysis and synthesis of information or data.

The strategic shift to flexi-learning represents one of the most serious threats to autonomy, we contend, posed by new managerialism in the FE sector. It is seen to strike at the heart of the professional's paradigm because it degrades the expertise underpinning the degree of autonomy within the labour process and which includes choices about pace, extent of digression and the other elements which characterise different teaching styles. If teaching is mainly about the 'imparting of knowledge', as the Principal appears to believe, then a computer can fulfil the teacher's role. While it could be argued that this represents a very narrow perception of flexi-learning, it remains the case that the Principal's view is that, at Cityshire, this mode of learning will be IT based.

Consequently, Derber's words of over a decade earlier, and originally used in the context of the US public service, may be applied to teaching in the UK further education sector:

> *While professionals are currently distinguished by unique technical autonomy, new information technologies, especially sophisticated generations of computers and microprocessors, have been discussed as a basis for mechanisation or routinisation of professional work and the undermining of professional monopolies of knowledge.*

(Derber, 1983: 335)

The intrusion of the market

The concept of the student as 'customer' (Du Gay & Salaman, 1992; Willmott, 1994; Parker & Jary, 1995) has further implications for lecturer control over the labour process. The lecturer/student relationship has traditionally rested on notions of common enterprise, cooperation and mutual responsibilities. The assumption was that the student would participate in a process of learning that was characterised by dialogue and a discourse between student and teacher which demanded student cooperation, engagement in group-related tasks, face-to-face student interaction and fulfilment of general course requirements by, for instance, attending classes and completing assignments.

A customer/supplier relationship is now beginning to displace the relationship outlined above. It has been suggested that in the case of the 'New Higher Education' the consumer/student has been used as a surrogate surveillance device (Parker & Jary, 1995: 326). Under the FEFCE's Charter for Further Education, colleges are now obliged to set up formal complaints procedures. Walsh (1995) argues that such procedures have been central to the new public management and represent one aspect of the move to 'marketisation', the individually based concept of citizenship and an assault on the power of professional bureaucracies.

However, there is a paradox in the fact that the adoption of market relations by organisations has often been the result of 'formal, centralised and bureaucratic compulsion' (Du Gay & Salaman, 1992: 620) and, in the case of FE, we witness the effective imposition of market relations by the bureaucracy of the FEFCE.

Taken at face value a formal complaints procedure may seem like a reasonable and democratic mechanism, designed to protect the student (customer) from unsatisfactory treatment at the hands of the college and its employees. However, the complaints procedure as constituted represents a potentially destructive instrument that could undermine the authority of lecturers in the perception of the student. Under the procedure, students are actively encouraged to complain, with the results that students have questioned lecturer competence on the basis of their perceptions of 'correct classroom activity', i.e. the lecturer's teaching methods, rather than the skill used for their execution.

Perhaps the most striking example of the new managerialism is the surveillance implicit in the attempt by management to measure performance in terms of quantifiable outcomes. This has found its expression in the proliferation of business plans and various quality assurance measures. Lecturers have been inundated with requests to complete records or provide lesson plans, complete questionnaires or to get students to complete questionnaires. The areas monitored by these measures range from student enrolment processes to the quality of the canteen service. Most of these activities are regarded by the lecturers as merely fruitless or irksome; 54.4% of lecturers responding to the survey regarded quality assurance research as 'not beneficial' and another 28% didn't know whether it was or not.

In conducting this performance measurement, management stress its importance in ensuring the quality of the service and responsiveness to the customer. The other side of this, however, is its negative effects on lecturer morale and Hoggett (1994) has argued that performance surveillance destroys trust and leads to those aspects of work which are not visible or not measurable becoming undervalued. This may, in turn, affect the quality of the service to the users. Therefore, in the context of the health of the long-term relationship between lecturer and student such a loss of self-esteem by the lecturer could have serious consequences. In the attitude survey, 93.1% of respondents reported a loss of morale between 1992 and 1994 with 70% of the sample falling into the category which we regard as constituting a 'serious' loss of morale. A recent study of further education lecturers by psychologists (Stead *et al.* 1995) found that full-time staff reported working an average of 43 hours per week, against their contract expectancy of 30 hours per week on duty at college [4] and that high levels of anxiety and depression existed in their sample. The inability of these staff to provide quality teaching was a major factor in producing stress levels where 43% scored high enough to be considered at borderline and clinical levels of anxiety. These authors conclude that organisations which disregard the relationship between perceptions of work overload and the decline in decision-making ability may have a dramatic affect on the future profitability and efficiency of their businesses.

The proletarianisation of academic labour?

Within the growing body of literature on changes in the public service sector, some analysts (Wilson, 1991; Trow, 1993), have developed a 'proletarianisation', 'de-skilling' or 'de-professionalisation' thesis to describe the undermining of the professional paradigm by the new managerialism. Writing in the context of Higher Education, and in particular the new universities, Wilson argues that academic proletarianisation has resulted from the 'degradation of work'. This involves the dilution of the quality of the teaching provision, the lowering of academic standards, the deterioration of lecturer pay and conditions and the erosion of professional status. Wilson, however, stops short of endorsing the deskilling thesis, arguing that jobs which have become deskilled within the academic structure have subsequently been displaced to administrative and clerical staff (Wilson, 1991: 258).

The comparison with the process occurring in HE is illuminating because it underlines the depth of the process currently taking place within FE. Casualisation is being institutionalised in the form of the ELS (Education Lecturing Services), a private agency set up to circumvent the financial problems college managements would otherwise experience as a result of the improved employment rights and redundancy payments of part-time lecturers (*The Guardian*, 7 March 1995: 8). At Cityshire a number of former part-time staff have been given fractional appointments as a result of changed employment rights, but the College now employs all of its remaining part-time lecturers through ELS. Casualisation can be seen as a method of increasing the flexibility of the workforce in the FE sector in order to achieve efficiency gains.

The process of deprofessionalisation in FE not only contains recognisable elements of the degradation of work, but also represents a systematic deskilling of the lecturer. The displacement of teacher contact time by the beginnings of IT-driven flexible learning; the loss of control over student management; the lowering of academic standards; the assessment of performance by external agencies; the prescriptive nature of, for example, GNVQ courses, and the loss of control over intellectual property support the argument that the FE lecturer is being systematically and comprehensively deskilled. Derber, writing in the context of the human service sector in the USA in 1983, identified the trend towards what he termed the 'ideological proletarianisation' of the professional. By this he meant:

... the appropriation of control by management over the goals and social purposes to which the work is put. Elements of ideological proletarianisation include powerlessness to define the final product of one's work, its disposition in the market and its uses in the larger society.

(Derber, 1983: 313)

This is regarded as less serious than 'technical proletarianisation', as control over core tasks is retained even as autonomy over overall organisational goals is lost (Kirkpatrick *et al.* 1996). Derber suggests that whereas 'technical proletarianisation', the loss of professional control over the labour process itself, had not taken place in this sector, there was none the less the possibility that this could happen. Proletarianisation theorists have proposed that the process could be facilitated by the introduction of new technologies and by the imposition of a management stratum which did not share the professional training of staff, was unsympathetic to aspirations towards professional autonomy, and would accept management systems which rationalise the deskilling of professional labour. Another important factor is change in the market situation of certain professional groups which may weaken their bargaining power and render them less capable of resisting the process. Of these he argues:

The most ominous market considerations apply to public sector professionals, such as teachers, social workers and many categories of local state and federal employees, who are extraordinarily vulnerable to the fiscal crises affecting all levels of government. The ensuing demand for new austerities and efficiencies in public service imply ... new managerial rationalisations, already apparent in new forms of quantified productivity controls imposed on social workers and teachers.

(Derber, 1983: 341)

The parallels of this analysis with the current position of FE lecturers is striking.

First, we can see the emergence of a new type of manager in FE operating with an apparently different value system from that of the academic staff. Secondly, the potential of the new information technologies to undermine the lecturers' labour process has been emphasised in this paper. Thirdly, we have argued that government education policy is designed to increase student numbers while lowering the level of unit funding. In our study 83.7% of respondents to the attitude survey reported a loss of job satisfaction during the period of the research and 53.4% reported a serious loss of job satisfaction. Of the respondents, 68.8% reported that they had experienced a loss of control over their teaching process during 1992–94. In essence, lecturers felt that they were being deprofessionalised through both the devaluation of their professional status and the loss of control over their labour process. The attitudes of staff at Cityshire would seem to support the idea that this particular body of professional employees are experiencing both 'ideological' proletarianisation and 'technological' proletarianisation through de-skilling. In other words, not only are they suffering degradation of work in terms of lower pay and fewer resources, but they are experiencing real attacks on their professional autonomy.

149

Conclusions

The deprofessionalisation of the lecturer is a direct outcome of government strategy within the FE sector. In order to prompt a significant expansion of further education, while simultaneously reducing unit costs, it has been necessary to intensify work in the colleges and this has been reflected in the dispute over new contracts. Pressure has been applied on the staff of colleges to comply with the demands of central government via a continued pay freeze on staff who elect not to sign the new contracts and on managers through the FEFCE's withholding or clawing back of funding.

Intensification of work can be seen in the increased teaching hours required of staff, although at Cityshire members of senior management see a future with greater emphasis on independent learning and increased dependence on educational technology which will undermine the professional autonomy of lecturers.

Whereas managers have defined increased quality in education in terms of providing a cost-effective product to a wider section of the community, staff regard this as a rationalisation for increasing throughput whilst cutting costs. The goals and values embraced by the 'new managers' are not shared by lecturing staff, who continue to uphold the values of public service professionalism. This clash of paradigms has led to both organisational dysfunction in the day-to-day delivery of the service at Cityshire, and to a bitter, if uneven, national dispute which is reflected at Cityshire in a continued refusal of the majority of staff to accept new contracts.

Marketisation has reconstituted the student as 'customer' and encouraged monitoring of lecturers through quality systems and complaints procedures. The customer has in turn taken on the role of manager, being in the unique position of being able to monitor and evaluate the hitherto hidden, expert and indeterminate aspects of the lecturer's role. What is new here is the shift from an informal evaluation of the lecturer to one which is formal, documented and public. At the same time lecturers are squeezed from the top by new managers: those whose role is to balance the budget, increase student numbers, generate income and satisfy the quality specifications of the FEFCE.

It has been argued (Kirkpatrick *et al.* 1996) that the imposition of new managerialism in the public sector has resulted in greater conflict where a separate management cadre was developed (as in the NHS) than where it was introduced through the professions (as in the case of university librarians). It would be difficult to argue that new managerialism in FE represents a case of the profession having accommodated to change in order to keep professional control. Rather, those who have become managers appear to have adopted a value system that reflects the new managerialism and have 'benefited' from the increased status that comes with the title 'manager'. Viewed from the perspective of the lecturer this group are seen as having set aside professional values, thus professional control has been lost.

It would nevertheless be a mistake to think that the only power that exists amongst 'professional' occupations is that which derives from the indeterminacy of work tasks.

Power can also be articulated through collective action and it may be that this kind of power has been gained as a result of the immediacy of the market in the sector. Lecturers continue to fight to maintain control over their labour process, to counter both deskilling and the degradation of work and a radical deterioration in their conditions of employment. Together these can be seen to represent the deprofessionalisation and the consequent 'proletarianisation' of this occupational group. That the traditional weapon of proletarians, the strike, has been employed with increasing regularity serves to both underline the degree to which lecturers are coming to terms with their changing status and the limitations of traditional forms of professional control within the sector.

Notes

[1] The authors are grateful to participants at the 1996 Labour Process conference, Aston University, where an earlier version of this paper was presented and to the anonymous referees whose diligence has contributed considerably to the coherence of this final version. However, the views expressed are those of the authors and any errors or omissions must be similarly attributed.

[2] Cityshire College is a pseudonym.

[3] The College Employers Forum (CEF) has since merged with the Association for Colleges (AFC) to produce the Association of Colleges (AoC).

[4] This should not be taken as suggesting that FE teachers have a contract expectancy of only 30 hours per week. No upper limit is placed on the hours that staff work on, for example, marking and preparation. However, a member of staff may be required to be available on college premises for 30 hours each week.

References

Braverman H (1974) *Labour and monopoly capital* Monthly Review Press

Burrage M & Torstendahl R (1990) *Professions in theory and history* Sage

Crompton R (1990) 'Professions in the current context' *Work Employment and Society* Special issue May, pp147–166

Dearing R (1994) 'Strategic planning in FE: the impact of incorporation' *Mendip Paper* (MP061) The Staff College

Derber C (1983) 'Managing professionals: ideological proletarianisation and post industrial labour' *Theory and Society* 12, pp309–341

Du Gay P & Salaman G (1992) 'The cult(ure) of the customer' *Journal of Management Studies* 29, pp615–33

Elliot G (1996) 'Educational management and the crisis of reform in further education' *Journal of Vocational Education and Training* 48, pp5–23

Farnham D & Horton S (eds) (1993) *Managing the new public services* Macmillan

Flynn N (1993) *Public sector management* Harvester Wheatsheaf

Gorringe R & Togood P (eds) (1994) 'Changing the culture of a college' *Coombe Lodge Report* 24 (3) The Staff College

Gunn L (1988) 'Public management: a third approach?' *Public Money and Management* Spring/Summer, pp21–25

Hoggett P (1994) 'New modes of control in the public services' *Management Research News* 17 (7/8/9), pp17–19

Kirkpatrick I & Martinez Lucio M (eds) (1995) *The politics of quality: management of change in the UK public sector* Routledge

Kirkpatrick I, Whipp R & Davies A (1996) 'New public management and the professions' in I Glover & M Hughes (eds) *The professional managerial class: contemporary British management in the pursuer mode* Avebury

Legge K (1989) 'Human resource management: a critical review' in S Storey (ed) *New perspectives on human resource management* Routledge

Major J (1989) *Public service management: the revolution in progress* The London Audit Commission

Metcalf L & Richards S (1987) *Improving public management* Sage

McGinty J & Fish J (1993) *Further education in the market place* Routledge

Miller H (1991) 'Academics and their labour process' in C Smith, D Knights & H Willmott (eds) *White-collar work* Macmillan, pp109–137

Nash I (1994) 'Funding formula punishes the cautious' *The Times Educational Supplement* 10 June

Parker M & Jary D (1995) 'The McUniversity: organisation, management and academic subjectivity' *Organization* 2, pp319–338

Pollitt C (1990) *Managerialism and the public services: the Anglo-American experience* Blackwell

Ritzer G (1993) *The McDonaldisation of society* Pine Forge

Rueschemeyer D (1983) 'Professional autonomy and the social control of expertise' in R Dingwall & P Lewis (eds) *The sociology of the professions* Macmillan

Stead B, Fletcher B & Jones F (1995) 'Relationships between workload, cognitive decision making and psychological well being' in *Proceedings of the British Psychological Society Occupation Psychology Conference* Eastbourne, January 1996

Stewart J & Walsh K (1992) 'Change in the management of public services' *Public Administration* 70, pp519–532

Trow M (1993) 'Managerialism and the academic profession' paper to The Quality Debate Conference, Open University

Walsh K (1995) 'Quality through markets' in A Wilkinson & H Willmott (eds) *Making quality critical* Routledge

Warner D & Crosthwaite E (1995) *Human resource management in higher and further education* Open University Press

Wilkinson A & Willmott H (eds) (1995) *Making quality critical* Routledge

Willmott H (1994) 'Managing the academics: commodification and control in the development of university education in the UK' paper to the 12th Annual Labour Process Conference, Aston University

Wilson T (1991) 'The proletarianisation of academic labour' *Industrial Relations Journal* 22, pp250–262

17. A Framework for Exploring Values in the FE Curriculum

Joint Churches Working Group

Introduction

This is the second in a series of three publications on the subject of shared values in FE, produced jointly by the Church of England Board of Education and the Methodist Church Division of Education and Youth...

The original report in September 1992 ('The Further Education Curriculum: An exploration into and identification of shared values in the FE provision') provided a number of reasons for the Church's interest in FE and outlined several examples of its growing ecumenical commitment over the past 25 years. To avoid unnecessary repetition it may be sufficient to quote from it one of the key elements of the churches' mission in FE colleges, which is:

> *To contribute to the pursuit of excellence in FE and have a concern for the spiritual, moral and personal values being communicated and developed through the whole curriculum and other aspects of college life.*

The Church is mindful of the historical secular nature of FE and the need for sensitivity towards those of other faiths, and those of none. This approach is borne out by the widespread acceptance and demand for copies of the initial report by the colleges, and by the many different ways in which they are using it. Examples of its use include: background reading for Governors; a resource for tutorial programmes; City and Guilds FE Teachers' Certificate Course 730; and curriculum development.

The Working Group, in its desire to build upon this success, decided to focus on the specific values issues confronting two discrete groups in the colleges:

- the Governors, Principals and Senior Management; and
- Middle Management and Course Team Leaders.

It was agreed to tackle this through a survey of a cross-section of colleges across the country, complemented by independent investigations by members of the Working Group in their own colleges, and the support of consultants...

The survey forms posed the following questions:

1. List *two* or *three* examples of difficult value judgements in which you are currently involved.
2. Focus on *one* particular example, describing the decision-making process and highlighting the issues involved.
3. If you have any further comments you would like to make, please state below...

The Working Group did not wish to convey the impression of prescribing values, which might be the case if the word 'guidelines' was retained, as proposed in the original recommendation...

During the course of the investigation it became evident that the survey would provide a 'framework' for understanding the issues being addressed in the colleges and, therefore, this should be reflected in the title of the report.

When the responses to the survey were analysed, a grouping of the issues under four general headings to form a framework for exploring the values in the curriculum appeared apt. The Working Group would like to suggest that this framework provides a helpful approach to such an exploration. The categories of issues are:

Group 1   Commerce-versus-Caring

Group 2   Valuing of Staff

Group 3   Valuing the Content of Learning Programmes

Group 4   Values in Teaching Methods and Management

(see Part Three)

The report is intended to serve at least two functions.

- The first objective is to enable Church Boards of Education, across the ecumenical spectrum, to have an insight into some of the curriculum issues on which they could express their concern.

- The second objective is to clarify for the colleges the churches' concern for FE.

It is hoped that the Christian lay presence in the general FE, tertiary and sixth form colleges will be encouraged by the churches to play a major part in this process.

PART ONE

The role of governors, principals and senior management

Knowing the price of everything and the value of nothing?

(after Oscar Wilde)

The implementation of the F and HE 1992 Act has led to the creation of a new independent FE sector free from the control of Local Authorities. From April 1993 the general FE, tertiary and sixth-form colleges became corporate institutions, taking responsibility for their own budget, management of buildings, resources, conditions of employment and salaries. Another feature has been the higher representation from local industry and commerce on the college Governing bodies.

Colleges are having to make difficult decisions which affect their range and quality of provision and where their resources should be directed. There is a growing need to generate income to supplement that received centrally from the Further Education Funding Council and other sources of revenue.

The ethos is becoming more akin to the world of business. The language and terminology is noticeably changing; education is a commodity to be marketed; students are customers and clients, and economic factors have the tendency to over-rule other considerations.

The Church has begun to appreciate the impact that Incorporation is making, and when it realises the extent of the challenges facing colleges, it will be in a better position to offer informed support to both staff and students. To this end the responses to the Working Group survey are illuminating.

Survey results on values issues

There were 44 responses from members of the senior management, including some Governors, in the 15 colleges which took part in the survey. [The seven major recurring issues that were raised (not in rank order) were as follows]:

1. The college mission statement

The degree of staff involvement in the process of producing a mission statement varied considerably between colleges.

The responses under this heading included the following observations:

- The drafting and reviewing of the mission statement has provided an opportunity for clarification of aims and a discussion with managers/governors/staff to establish a consensus. The demands of time set by the Further Education Funding Council (FEFC) meant a restriction on consultation which did, in some cases, mean a loss of 'ownership' and a sense of lack of involvement. To overcome any loss in ownership, some principals have sent out regular newsletters keeping staff informed throughout Incorporation and these will continue.

- Some colleges took senior management away from the campus so that they could concentrate totally on the mission/vision statement. There is obviously a perceived dichotomy between the business needs of the college and the demands for educating individuals and promoting a caring environment for students and teachers. The contribution from business-orientated governors had a hard-cutting edge and provided different perspectives. Teachers may feel undervalued if education is undervalued in a business-orientated environment. Although the financial advantages, which are derived from a business-like focus, are welcomed, teachers do not always equate this with the educational and caring demands which are placed on staff and pupils. It is to be hoped that the mission statement informs staff of the direction the college is taking and why it is moving in this direction. Thus there will be key targets and the vision to work towards.

- A number of colleges have decided to go for the Investor in People status ... because it is all about valuing people and improving communication. This has reached out to the non-teaching staff and has largely been well received by them.

Example

A college mission statement:

The College aims to meet the needs of the community by providing a quality service which achieves positive outcomes by:

- ensuring proper guidance and induction to new students to the College
- providing excellent on-course support in a safe and attractive learning environment
- working closely with schools, parents, employers and local interests to serve their needs and maintain the broad waterfront of provision
- encouraging and facilitating staff to operate with maximum professional and personal effectiveness in meeting College aims
- making continuous improvements in efficiency and effectiveness in its use of resources
- demonstrating a commitment to quality through all aspects of its operations.

2. The entitlement curriculum

The entitlement curriculum, particularly the cost of providing 16–19-year-old full-time students with opportunities above and beyond their core programme of study and essential pastoral care and learning support is an issue which is currently being addressed. (The Charter for FE was published in September 1993 by the Department for Education.)

If one assumes that total resources are fixed, then the more that is provided for 16–19-year-old full-time students, the less there will be available for other groups of students. A further dilemma concerns the quality of the educational experience. If full-time students are timetabled for an unreasonable number of hours each week, they will thus be denied the opportunity to become more self-directed and personally responsible for achieving their educational goals. A balance must be maintained.

An extract from a statement of student entitlement published by one college which follows may provide a useful example – from this a clear pattern emerges of what a student may expect and what the college proposes to deliver.

Example

... all full-time students will be entitled to:

- A Tutor who will be available to discuss progress and attainment. He/she will maintain a written record of the tutorial, signed by both parties, at least once a term.
- The development of numeracy, written and oral communication, information technology, and personal and social skills.
- An Alternative Studies programme which provides students with the opportunity to undertake activities and studies to complement or contrast with their main programme of activity, including the opportunity to learn a modern foreign language.
- Vocational experience – through work placement shadowing or simulations or via industry-linked activities, visits, talks etc., and a consideration of changing economic and social contexts.

3. Efficiency in monetary terms

Decisions concerning efficiency in monetary terms affect which courses are run and the number of students taught, e.g. choices between high cost (practical, vocational workshop-based) courses and lower cost (classroom-based activity).

One college presented the following illustration:

Example

	National Av'ge 91/92	College 91/92
Balance of expenditure:		
Employees	77%	79%
Supplies & Services	14%	11%
Premises	9%	9%

The proportion of the College's resources spent on supplies and services (students) is low compared to the national average, and given the low resourcing level of the College, this problem is exacerbated. However, given the overall resource situation, to direct resources from staff budgets to student budgets is not an easy option; indeed, it could be argued that decreasing staffing budgets directly affects the quality of service to the student.

A recommendation is being made to Governors that over time a higher proportion of the College resource is directed at supplies and services for students, e.g. equipment, facilities, library, guidance, counselling, environment, access, learner entitlement.

Consultations are ongoing with staff unions on this important issue, but of course there is a great deal of uncertainty and concern on the part of staff over independence, so the climate is not good for any concessions (even for the benefit of students).

4. Competition versus collaboration

This issue concerns the advantages and disadvantages of a market-place style of promotion.

The premium on expansion, set by the FEFC, requires colleges to market themselves to those students who might otherwise attend neighbouring schools and colleges. These other schools and colleges might suffer as a consequence of these marketing techniques. The effect on a small school sixth form could be disastrous and lead to an impoverishment of education for those that remain.

Example

A sixth form college might have had a policy of collaboration with a local FE college to offer general education (A levels, GCSEs) whilst they offered vocational education and training. Now there is an open market and they will be in competition. How far should the sixth form college go along the vocational route in response to the other college offering A levels? Duplication will not serve students' interests. The college, after involving all staff in the decision-making process, is:

- to offer GNVQ Level 3 (vocational A levels) in 3 areas
- to increase the A level provision and so make it more attractive
- to continue to counsel students according to what is perceived as their educational needs rather than the needs of the institution (i.e. to apply to the *other* college where appropriate)
- not to recruit overtly from neighbouring 11–18 schools, but to respond to invitations (to address parents etc).

The overriding concern must obviously be for the needs of the individual student. However, sensitivity is needed to address the fears of staff who may feel their jobs are at stake.

Example

This example of a similar issue was offered by another college:

The College has asked the City Council to withdraw from the management of the gym and dance studio which were formerly part of the school/college and which the City Council now let to the public during community time as part of the facilities of the new Sports Centre.

The County Council handled responsibility for these two spaces during the City Council evenings, weekends and holidays, without consultation with the College, when they were agreeing that the City would staff and manage the new Sports Centre.

The College undoubtedly has much greater need of these spaces now that it has grown substantially and the range of its work has increased. However, if the College took complete control of them it would probably result in a reduction in public use.

Process followed:
- Principal writes to City Council and Education Associations
- Board makes request for management control
- Association Board representative visits college to see problem
- City Council Officer makes informal visit to college to discuss compromise but insists they will fall back on legal agreement if necessary
- Meeting with Senior City Council Officers to be held.

The issue is – should the College try to insist on ownership and control of the spaces and gain the benefit of extra use and lettings income or should it allow the City Council to manage this in accordance with their priorities?

5. *Staffing levels: full-time experienced staff being replaced by part-time staff because of cost*

The possible replacement of experienced full-time staff by part-timers because they are less expensive is a decision which causes much concern. The decision-making process starts with a numerical exercise 'revenue against costs' to establish what efficiency gains have to be made in order to sustain the required growth. Management have to establish needs, taking into account sizes of groups, learning support and counselling required, age, 'profile' of group (learning difficulties, neighbourhood, ethnic background etc). Tutorial support in particular requires experienced full-time staff. Some compromise may be reached by agreeing to pay part-time staff for additional support duties, beyond the contracted 'class contact' hours.

Quality provision must of course be maintained but greater burdens may be imposed on remaining full-time staff which in turn affects morale. Whether or not there should be funding to reward effective teaching developments and to maintain quality in the light of increased numbers is a decision being discussed.

The access to colleges for students with severe physical and learning difficulties may be restricted because of lack of funds for care assistants.

More flexible learning can be used to deal with financial restrictions. This means less staff input, with students taught in larger numbers and then split for smaller tutorials and given student-centred packages. The type of student and his/her needs and interests must be considered. More students need to be educated to the 'self-find' instead of 'staff-feed' approach.

6. Pastoral curriculum can seem to be under threat

Some senior management offered the following comments:

- It is sometimes difficult to persuade staff that guidance, counselling and tutorial sessions are a valuable support for students and to encourage staff to train if they are unsure of their own capabilities. The pastoral curriculum is the backbone of Further Education, and it is reassuring that it is being given a high profile by FEFC. Often, however, this aspect of the curriculum is regarded as a side issue irrelevant to vocational teaching. The needs of the students should be paramount.

- Often such change as a higher profile for guidance, counselling and tutorials is not achieved until it is 'forced' by the demands of an external organisation such as BTEC or FEFC. Change, therefore, is a long-winded process because staff are not always convinced of the need until some external organisation makes them 'own' it for themselves. However, change often has to be achieved very quickly to meet external pressures and this in turn causes stress.

- Every effort is made to include as many staff as possible in the decision-making process and to provide a broader vision of student need.

7. Student discipline in a post-16 college where rules are not always clearly defined and where individual cases can be varied and complex

One principal raised the issue of the college's responsibility to the parents.

FE aims to provide a learning environment that gives 16–19-year-old students the opportunity to 'own' their own learning and assume responsibility for their own decisions. At times a balance has to be achieved between the civil liberties of the student (she or he being given the responsibility for their own actions and therefore maintaining confidentiality to that student) with the legal responsibilities and 'right-to-know' of the parents. Below the age of 18 the emphasis is on the parent. This can be quite a dilemma for the college management. Wherever possible the 'right-to-know' is restricted to the student and yet the decision to inform the parents involves a balance of judgement.

If the offence is illegal obviously the parents are informed; if the offence is a matter of poor work, attendance, tomfoolery and so on, there is no list of offences to which to refer. Dealing with students whose work/attendance is poor for a variety of reasons can take up a lot of staff time. Should such students be supported or is the matter resolved by asking them to leave?...

PART TWO

The role of middle management and course team leaders

Living up to expectations

There is a general consensus amongst staff who operate at this level that too much responsibility is devolved down, with fewer resources and time to manage the rate of curriculum changes.

The management of budgets and the demands of administration appear to conflict with the sustaining of the quality of education, tutoring and personal development through the curriculum.

The responses to the survey clearly reveal a contrasting scale of issues to that of the senior management team.

Survey results on values issues

In this section of the survey there were 52 responses from the members of staff in the 15 colleges...

The following is a selection of more detailed examples from staff who are most in contact with students and are at the delivery point of the college curriculum. The replies were often written in the first person and are quoted thus without commentary. [The five major recurring issues were as follows]:

1. Tutorial system

Importance and wide reaching responsibility of the tutor; and the successful implementation of the role: pastoral, disciplinary, personal.

Student discipline – the role of tutor/PAL (Programme Area Leader)

One Programme Area Leader explains the procedure at her college.

The College has a set procedure which has to be followed in all cases where a Tutor, Course Director or PAL has to deal with a student who needs to be reminded of his/her 'contract' with the College. The process is clear, but there are often many issues wrapped up in this process which are not easily untangled.

Example

A student who is attending most classes but missing one or two on a regular basis:

This student is quickly spotted by the lecturers.

Notes of poor attendance are sent to the Tutor and the Tutor will talk to the individual, making a note of the conversation on the appropriate form. The student will usually promise to try harder. Issues that are raised by this first meeting could include:

a) the student is not happy with the class – the relationship between the teacher/student may not be good

b) the class may be at a time when the student wants to be with 'friends' on other courses who may be free at that time

c) the demands of the subject may be too hard for the student to meet – this is made worse by continued absence.

The Tutor will feed back to the PAL any concerns regarding issues of timetable/ quality of delivery etc. The PAL can arrange to try to amend the timetable/see the appropriate member of staff. This may be a solution. It may be possible to transfer a student on to another course, although in most cases students resist this because it indicates a 'demotion'. More commonly, a student does not attend a range of classes. The procedure is followed, the student is seen and put on Report. A student may not remember to carry around the Report, or may not get it signed. If there are difficulties the Tutor will refer the student to the PAL. The admission card may be blocked so that the student will be referred to the PAL at the time they next attend. At this stage the issues that can often turn up concern the background of the student. Conversations and outcomes are recorded on the appropriate forms and a formal letter is written to the student and posted. Quite often the old pattern quickly re-establishes itself and the student will be referred again to the PAL.

If appointments are broken or the student has not attended for some time it will be deemed that the student has withdrawn from the course, and a letter to that effect will be sent to the student.

In some cases there will follow an appeal from a parent, social worker, children's home director or probation officer that we give the student another opportunity to rejoin the programme of study. This is often the time when the real dilemma begins. The student has had many opportunities – do you give him/her another chance?

Considerations:

a) What will they do if they are not allowed to attend college?

b) They may have no other opportunity to change their behaviour or gain qualifications...

c) One can have sympathy for a parent/social worker etc. who spends time with the student outside college and wants to help.

d) Some students respond very well and can make good progress, gain qualifications and make good progression to other courses.

e) Even if the student does not achieve the successful outcome, they will have gained from being on a course and working with others.

However:

a) What about the morale of the tutors – should they not be supported?

b) Maintaining discipline/good practice with existing students is difficult if 'exceptions' are made.

c) There is a procedure in operation within the college.

Class size and tutorial provision

A lecturer expresses concern for part-time students in this response:

- No specific time is made available for tutorials in part-time classes, but this is often the environment where a time allocation would be helpful, both because of time pressure and because of the particular pressures on part-time students (especially in a recessionary environment). Pressure from heads of department to increase class size (e.g. 20 in a professional post-A level course this term) means that less time is available for attention to individual students, both for academic and pastoral provision and care. One feels that it is one's professional and personal responsibility to give students time outside formal classes to provide this academic, pastoral and career support, but this clearly leads to conflict with other classes and other professional and personal commitments.

2. Tension between teaching and administration

- *How can a balance of time be achieved?*
- *Which has priority?*

The feelings of staff are illustrated by these personal comments:

- It is often difficult to prioritise tasks – sometimes I have felt that it is my preparation for teaching which has taken lowest priority and therefore suffered.

- I sometimes feel guilty at having covered classes in order to attend student development etc. connected with my cross-college administration.

- I am often frustrated because the cross-college administration role requires a very flexible teaching timetable – the need to be available at most times. This is impossible with a regular class contact timetable and often involves complicated juggling.

- It is often difficult to convince other teaching staff of the value of time spent on administration tasks to do with the quality process – at least I do get some time (remission) to carry out my role. Many teaching staff feel they are just being asked to do more and more administration and are unsure what their role is any more.

A case study which highlights tensions between teaching and administration:

Example

With ever-increasing pressure to offer new and updated courses, time available (after preparation, delivery and marking) is increasingly tight. The administration side of the job includes cover for sick staff. A current problem is arranging to cover two full-time members of staff and four part-time members of staff for two days whilst they are on a course. As the section includes only three full-time staff (I am included in this number), three Associate Lecturers and part-timers, this is extremely difficult. It has taken a great deal of time and persuasion to organise sufficient cover and one class may yet have to be cancelled. There is very little goodwill left amongst staff as far as covering for sick colleagues is concerned, or covering at all for that matter.

As many staff as possible have to attend the course in order to achieve a training award which is necessary for training delivery in the future.

3. Staffing levels and size of classes

- *Use of part-time staff cover for absent colleagues*
- *Reduction of library service and support staff*
- *Less time for the individual student.*

A Director of Studies describes a situation which arose because of the reduction in the number of full-time staff:

Example

The section for which I am responsible has identified a Higher National Diploma in Theatre and Education which could be very well resourced by existing staff and would not make *undue* additional demands on existing facilities. As I teach 16 hours a week on a very demanding course and have recently lost one full-time and one half-time post, my administrative load has increased considerably and I have had to rely on a member of part-time staff, admittedly politically very experienced, to undertake initial negotiations with the Higher Education Institute with whom we will be offering the new course. He has not required, and certainly has not been offered, a fee for his time.

When it came to actually writing the course, classes had to be cancelled and part-time lecturers invited to attend, with no hope of offering them a fee for doing so, though the majority are freelance and presumably could have been earning elsewhere.

4. Special needs

How far should resources be allocated and buildings re-modelled to admit students with special needs?

One lecturer poses the following questions:

- To what extent should a college spend money on providing facilities for disabled people?

- For example, should every classroom/teaching area be fitted with a loop system?

- Should buildings be structurally altered to provide toilets which are accessible for disabled students who use a wheelchair?

- What are the implications for other students in the college and their ability to accept such a diversity of students?

For teaching staff, there are questions about the ability to provide classes which do not discriminate against any of the students. Is it too restrictive if staff do not show videos to the group because one of them would not see what was happening?

5. Core skills

Delivery by qualified staff is important.

A course team leader writes:

The issues involved extend beyond the value judgement to practicalities, e.g. the need to fill timetables of full-time staff in other sections; the changing nature of qualifications and the part that core and communication skills has in these.

Example

The decision-making process presents no problem, as I believe that core skills should be a compulsory part of education – if we were a training establishment perhaps not!

In 'helping' others to make the decision the steps involved have included:
- building up a thoroughly professional, appropriately qualified team of staff
- presenting information to Senior Management to seek support by making and implementing a policy decision
- presenting information and discussing with other Sector Heads the issues
- supporting a core skills investigation project
- discussing at every opportunity with any involved parties the need for core and communication skills appropriately delivered
- supporting the core and communication skills team to maintain and improve quality and encourage development.

PART THREE

A framework for grouping values issues

The issues raised in the survey by, on the one hand, Governors, Principals and Senior Management, and, on the other, Middle Management and Course Team Leaders, may be grouped into four common categories to form a framework for the exploration of shared values. [This is expressed as a table in Figure 1 opposite.]

Governors, Principal and Senior Management	Middle Management and Course Team Leaders
Group 1: Commerce-versus-Caring	
Competition-versus collaboration. Efficiency in monetary terms. Access for non-fee payers. Imposition of an entrepreneurial culture. Reviewing the mission statement. Provision for special needs students.	Open recruitment and league tables. Education-versus-training. Measurable results-versus-personal development. Effect of finance on curriculum. Special needs.
Group 2: Valuing Staff	
Staffing levels. The effect of change on staff. Lack of resources for staff development. Involvement of staff in decision-making and communication. Maintaining quality of teaching staff. Internal promotion processes. Effect of industrial unrest and staff dissatisfaction.	Quality of tutorial systems. Staffing levels and size of classes. Staffing appraisal. Equal opportunities. Decision-making without consultation. Needs of individual students and that of the class and staff.
Group 3: Valuing the Content of Learning Programmes	
Pastoral curriculum under threat. Emphasis upon 16–19-year-old students. Clash between short-term and long-term benefits. Questioning the values of tutorial and counselling provision.	Core skills. Diversity of attitudes to 'value added' elements of academic and vocational programmes. Importance of spiritual, moral and personal development.
Group 4: Values in Teaching Methods and Management	
Use of packaged learning. Environment-versus-equipment. Managing change. Investors in People status. Governors may not understand the educational dimension to the college provision.	Tension between teaching and administration. Student-centred or teacher-centred learning. Planning problems with GNVQs. Discipline of students and developing learner's responsibility.

Figure 1 Framework for grouping values issues

Reflections

In the majority of FE sector colleges there is no obvious starting point for the exploration of values within the curriculum as in schools, where religious and moral education and collective worship is a statutory requirement... The framework of the survey findings as set out in this report do suggest that there are certain questions which might be discussed by ... those within the colleges who have a concern and responsibility for promoting quality and values... These might include:

1. Are the values expressed in the mission statement to be seen in the college's statement(s) on student entitlement?

2. Is there a specific mention of the importance of personal development in the entitlement statement?

3. Is there provision for students with special needs?

4. Do the local churches or other religious groups play an active role within the college?

5. Do the staff within the college feel valued and supported? How can this be assessed?

6. Does the college reach out to the whole community?

7. How far does the college respond to 'market forces' rather than the needs of individuals?

8. Does the local community value the management and the ethos of the college?

9. Are there particular theological perspectives on the values-framework which the churches could share with the colleges?